"As a mom currently raising a child w[...] comfort. As a pastor's wife, seeking to [...] ties, I found this book a guide. As a foll[...] [...] loved, helped, and healed people with disabilities, I found this book a gospel-rich resource. And finally, as a former student of Dr. Hulshof, having been a teenage new believer/fly on the wall back when he was grading my Bible verse tests and walking through the pain and uncertainty of his son's diagnosis, I found this book a joy. Dr. Hulshof's book, *Jesus and Disability*, will be a blessing for parents and church leaders seeking to love and make disciples as Jesus did."

—**Scarlet Hiltibidal**, speaker, and author of *Afraid of All the Things: Tornadoes, Cancer, Adoption, and Other Stuff You Need the Gospel For*

"What Chris Hulshof has accomplished in *Jesus and Disability* is head-turning! Engaging a subject that is generally treated topically, he rightfully places our response to disability where it truly belongs—in the character of Christ. The early chapters laid a methodical foundation for the outstanding 'wait for it' practical applications at the end of the book. *Jesus and Disability* was solidly biblical, well researched, and incredibly useful. I will be recommending this book for years to come."

—**Stephanie O. Hubach**, research fellow in disability ministries, Covenant Theological Seminary, and author of *Same Lake, Different Boat: Coming Alongside People Touched by Disability*

"There are many guides on how to make churches more inclusive for people with disabilities, but not all of them point us to our ultimate example—Jesus. In *Jesus and Disability*, Chris shows us how Jesus interacted with the disabled throughout the Gospels. We see his care, concern, and compassion, and we also see his inclusion and empowerment. After their encounters with Christ, people with disabilities were welcomed into their faith communities and given a mission to fulfill. The same is true today—our churches can follow his example by welcoming those who are often ostracized and empower them to use their gifts to build up the church. I'm so thankful for Chris's work in this area and the example he provides for us through his research and experience."

—**Sandra Peoples**, special-needs ministry consultant, Southern Baptists of Texas Convention, and author of *Unexpected Blessings: The Joys and Possibilities of Life in a Special-Needs Family*

JESUS AND DISABILITY

JESUS AND DISABILITY

A Guide to Creating an
Inclusive Church

CHRIS H. HULSHOF

ACADEMIC
NASHVILLE, TENNESSEE

Jesus and Disability
Copyright © 2022 by Chris Hulshof

Published by B&H Academic
Nashville, Tennessee

All rights reserved.

ISBN: 978-1-5359-9889-5

Dewey Decimal Classification: 259.4
Subject Heading: CHURCH WORK WITH THE
HANDICAPPED / LEADERSHIP / HANDICAPPED

For Becky and Connor.
I can't imagine a better journey than ours.

CONTENTS

ACKNOWLEDGMENTS

Thank you to the faculty at Southeastern Baptist Theological Seminary who allowed me the freedom to pursue disability-related topics in each of your classes during my studies there. This flexibility enabled me to think through and develop much of what has made its way into this book.

I am extremely appreciative for Dr. Ken Coley and his wisdom and council. Our discussions on the need for a practical model of disability-inclusive church ministry encouraged me to produce something that would assist those who are trying to make a kingdom difference in disability ministry. I appreciate the many ways you have poured into both me and my studies over the years.

To Dr. James Porowski, thank you for taking the time after our classes to encourage and support me. Some of the things I learned from you can be found on the pages of this book. Still others are now implemented in my classes at Liberty University.

I am grateful to Dr. Greg Lawson for mentoring me through the doctoral and dissertation process that led to this book. You were the first faculty member to come alongside me and encourage me to passionately pursue my interest in disability-related research. You were a constant source of encouragement and direction. Through course work and research, our conversations have shaped more than just this book.. Indeed, you have left an indelible mark on both my life and ministry. Your passion for Christ and his church truly is contagious.

Finally, to my students, in more ways than you will ever realize, you have made me a better student, researcher, professor, and communicator. Thank you for taking my Theology of Suffering and Disability class and for having a heart for the largest unreached people group in the world.

INTRODUCTION

There is nothing like looking, if you want to find
something. . . . You certainly usually find something, if you
look, but it is not always quite the something you were after.

J. R. R. TOLKIEN, *THE HOBBIT*

I'm not sure what you are looking for, but I am confident that you are
looking for something. That's the reason you picked up this book. Very
few people are interested in disability-related literature purely for enjoyment
reading. So, my guess is that you are hoping to find something or learn
something about disability-inclusive leadership on the following pages.

My interest in disabilities falls into three categories. Disability studies
are of personal, academic, and professional concern to me. I am the father of
an adolescent boy whose life is marked by disability. As such, I am familiar
with the daily struggles of accessibility and acceptability when it comes to
those who are disabled.

I am also an ordained Baptist pastor. I love the church and want to see
the church be better when it comes to the welcome and affirmation she
extends to the disabled. As a teenager, I was deeply involved in my local

church. Some of the most meaningful relationships in my life at that time came from the church. However, the same cannot be said about my son's involvement in our local church. To be sure, he enjoys going to church, and the volunteers do a great job looking out for him. Nevertheless, the most meaningful relationship that he has there is with the aide (or buddy) that he spends the hour with. He has virtually no peer-to-peer interaction. I want our church to do better. I want the global church to do better. It is my hope that this book helps pastors and church leaders be more aware of how to foster a disability-inclusive community of faith.

Disability literature and research is also an academic concern of mine. Indeed, most of what you will read on the following pages represents content that is drawn from my dissertation on disability-inclusive leadership. As I researched, read, and wrote for the dissertation, it became clear that there was a hole in the existing disability literature. While there seems to be no shortage of writers contributing content to the field of disability studies, most of what continues to be put out is more personal or experiential. It was my desire then (and still is now) to fill a little of that gap with an academic survey of primary biblical texts dealing with disability. More specifically, I want to show how Jesus's involvement with the disabled can be instrumental in laying the foundation for disability-inclusive church leadership.

Finally, as a professor, two of my regular teaching assignments are Inductive Bible Study and Theology of Suffering and Disability. I love teaching students how to study the Bible almost as much as I love helping them explore the practical and theological concerns of suffering and disability. In some sense, this book represents both of these academic interests. The pages that follow provide a methodical survey of select healing miracles of Jesus. These miracles are examined using a biblically faithful hermeneutic.

Each semester I also have the opportunity to engage and encourage students with the truth of God's Word as it relates to disability concerns. I have found that there is a generation of students who are eager to find ways to come alongside the disabled and provide meaningful physical, social, and spiritual assistance. Indeed, one reason I have hope that the future for those who are disabled is brighter than the present is because of the students I meet every day.

Broadly speaking, the material found on the pages of this book was shaped by the classroom experience. There is a blend of Bible study technique and classroom discussion as it relates to disability-inclusive leadership. Christian leadership rests on the solid foundation of God's Word. This is no less important when it comes to leadership focused on including those who are disabled.

I am not sure what it is you are looking for and why that lead you to this book. It is my hope that somewhere between the personal, academic, and professional content presented here, you will find the encouragement to lead like Jesus when it comes disability inclusion.

(1)

Laying the Groundwork for Disability-Inclusive Leadership

I remember the day I found out a person could live life with half of a brain. My wife and I had just received the diagnosis that our son had infantile epilepsy. The diagnosis did not surprise us. For three months after he was born, we suspected that something was not right, and we were sure that he was having seizures. We tried to get his pediatrician to understand what we were seeing in our son's behavior; however, she assured us that his "spasms" were reflexes common to newborns and that, as first-time parents, we were worrying too much.

My wife had the brilliant idea of recording a day in our son's life in hopes of capturing one of these spasmatic episodes. When she did, we felt we had more than enough evidence to show the pediatrician exactly what we were seeing. Armed with our video, we showed up for his next appointment ready to present our evidence that we were not overreacting first-timers and that there was something wrong with our son. However, no video would be needed during that visit. While we were in the appointment room with the doctor, our son had one of his daily seizures. The pediatrician immediately recognized what was going on and sent us on to the emergency room.

The next months were filled with more doctor's appointments, tests, and specialists' consultations than seemed imaginable. The end result was a confirmation of what he had suspected since his birth—our son was an epileptic. The doctor assured us that there was a good part to this diagnosis in that all of the bad brain tissue was confined to one side of our son's brain. This meant that if medicine couldn't control the seizures then brain surgery, extensive brain surgery to remove half of his brain, should work.

The next two years were difficult on many levels. We tried medicine, diets, and a number of small brain surgeries in an effort to eliminate the bad brain tissue that was causing the epileptic seizures in our son. With all that modern science had available to us, we were never able to get his seizures under control. So, right around the time of his second birthday, our son went through a functional hemispherectomy. This procedure left him with half of a functioning brain.

Today, our teenage son lives with the residual effects from this surgery. He has developmental delays in the physical, mental, and social aspects of life. His condition has led to significant changes in the way that my wife and I do life. Our lives do not look like the lives of our friends and neighbors. While disability directly impacts one member of a family, it affects every member of the family. We have learned the value of getting our bearings before going into a new situation. Since some places are not equipped for the disabled and certain situations are not opportune for them, we know the need to be as strategic as possible in these encounters.

Sadly, one such place we discovered that seemed to be neither concerned nor equipped for those who are disabled was the church. While I realize that this may not be true of your church, it has seemed to be a common theme with churches I have encountered over the past eighteen years. Marginal attention and resources are allotted to accommodate the disabled. Thus, when a disabled family decides to attend church, they have a better chance of finding a ministry that is "building the airplane as they are flying" rather than a church that has thought disability ministry through and is waiting with open arms to welcome those who are disabled and their families. A church that is purposefully strategic in their approach to the disabled proudly proclaims, "We have been expecting you. We are so glad you are here!"

I was reminded of this reality while reading an unfortunate account for a family with a disabled child in the book *Same Lake, Different Boat*. In it, Stephanie O. Hubach tells the story of a friend who brought her disabled son to a small-town hospital emergency room. This child had suffered a seizure and injured his mouth and tongue. He was in need of immediate help. The emergency room physician looked over the child and determined there was nothing he could do. It was beyond his experience and expertise. However, he did not consult other staff or doctors. He did not even propose treatment at another hospital. He simply sent the mother and her son on their way. This lack of concern for proper health care resulted in the boy needing weeks of medical treatment in a different hospital for his damaged tongue and mouth. Hubach summarizes her response to this story:

> When I first heard this tale, a myriad of emotions swelled up within me. The hospital's response—so obviously inappropriate and inhumane—engendered intense feelings of disbelief and indignation. "Isn't a hospital supposed to be a refuge of hospitality, a place of welcoming care for everyone in need of medical attention? How could anyone possibly do that to another human being in such apparent need?" And then it struck me: This story is an ugly but accurate parable of what we do—at times—in the church. Sometimes we forget that the church is not a country club for members but a hospital for sinners of all different stripes, with all different types of needs. And when we forget this, our response will probably be to shut the door: "Members Only. We can't deal with this."[1]

---

[1] Stephanie O. Hubach, *Same Lake, Different Boat: Coming Alongside People Touched by Disability* (Phillipsburg, NJ: P&R, 2006), 152.

Hubach's observation is correct regarding those who are disabled. It is still too commonplace for Christians who suffer from impairment to find themselves marginalized within the church.

This marginalization runs counter to the heart of God and his design for the church. The Scriptures establish God's compassion for the disabled as well as his desire for their inclusion in the household of faith. The Old Testament demonstrates this compassion and desire through narrative and instruction. In the New Testament, the life and teaching of Jesus Christ displays his Father's position on disabilities. This affirmation is primarily evidenced through his numerous encounters with the disabled. Furthermore, the apostles practiced the compassion and inclusion they learned from Jesus. One example of their practice is Peter's interaction with the lame man in Acts 3:1–10. This biblical and theological trajectory for disabilities provides the impetus for the contemporary church to be a standard bearer of compassion and inclusion.

Sadly, church leaders have been ill-prepared for those with disabilities who are part of their congregation. This problematic oversight creates an ecclesiastical climate where leaders must self-educate on disabilities, disability ministry, and disability-inclusive leadership. Resources that address these concerns from a biblical perspective are scant. At best, the church pastor must investigate educational offerings on disability and attempt to modify the material so that it is suitable both personally and congregationally. These efforts point to the pastor's desire to be a hospital for the hurting. At worst, the church leader deems the situation as awkward and the risk of embarrassment greater than the reward of potential inclusion. Thus, the marginalization of the disabled and the continued country club mentality persist within his church.

It is because of this country club mentality that I hope this book will meet a current need in church leadership and church ministry. It is my aim that this book addresses the biblical and theological need for disability-inclusive church leadership. For when a church is led by a disability-inclusive pastor, it will translate into a church where disability ministry is founded on the truth of Scripture and carried out with both the

Great Commission and the Great Commandment in mind. To that end, the material here represents a lexical, syntactical, structural, rhetorical, and theological survey of Jesus's interaction with the disabled as recorded in the Gospels. These five tools of exegesis are the best way to "dig deeper" into God's Word so that one can discover the timeless meaning of the text and then make timely application.

I believe that two implications will surface through this selective survey of Jesus's encounters with those who are disabled. First, it will uncover what the Bible presents with regard to Jesus's leadership style as he interacted with those who are disabled. Second, it will demonstrate how church leaders can incorporate the conclusions of this biblical survey into their own ministries as well as the body life of the churches they are serving.[2] Thus, this book will have the earmarks of orthodoxy and orthopraxy. Generally speaking, orthodoxy referrers to what one believes, while orthopraxy refers to how one practices or lives out what they believe.

---

[2] Body life: "that warm fellowship of Christian with Christian which the New Testament calls koinonia, and which was an essential part of early Christianity." Ray C. Stedman, *Body Life* (Grand Rapids: Discovery House, 1972, 2017), chap. 10.

The church is not a business establishment, where those who are hired to work in it and for it are assigned tasks based on what they are good at or what they bring to the table. In such a scenario, value is tied to one's skill and performance. Instead, the church is a body, with Christ as its head (Rom 12:4–6a; Eph 4:1–13). Each member of this body is valuable not because of his or her skills or performance but because of who all the members belong to—Christ, the head of the body. Stedman put it this way: "When Paul speaks of the church as a body; he makes it clear that no one joins that body except by a new birth, through faith in Jesus Christ. There is no other way into this body. Once a person becomes a part of that body, every member has a contribution to make. As each member works at the task God has given him to do, the whole body functions as intended." Stedman, chap. 7.

Thus, there are no spectators, sideliners, or benchwarmers in the body of Christ. Each member has been gifted by God to make a needed and valuable contribution to the body of Christ and to warmly interact with other members of the body. In this way, members are a part of the body of Christ and participate fully in the life of this body.

Why Study the Scriptures with an Eye toward Disability-Inclusive Leadership?

There are four reasons for undertaking a study of the Scriptures that investigates disability concerns and leadership as they are addressed in God's Word. First, the number of people who have been diagnosed with a disability continues to increase. Brault presents some staggering statistics about disability in the United States. In 2010 approximately 56.7 million people were listed as having a disability. Of this number, 38 million people have been diagnosed as having a severe disability. Further, there are 12.3 million people who are six years old or older that will need assistance with at least one of their daily activities because of a disability. When it comes to children, the statistics are equally overwhelming. There are 5.2 million children under the age of fifteen who have been diagnosed with a disability. For 1.7 million of these children, the disability has been classified as intellectual or developmental. These numbers also translate into a great educational need. The "1.6 million children who reported receiving special education services" underscore this educational need.[3]

Second, those with disabilities are often excluded from the church or marginalized by the church. The ostracism of the disabled by the church is something noted by Bill Amstutz, president of the disability ministry known as Shepherds Ministry. In an interview with Mission Network News, Amstutz asserts that while the church may have changed its architecture, it often has not altered its attitude. As a result of this attitudinal barrier, opportunities for the disabled to hear the gospel are much slower to develop.[4]

Third, much that is expressed on inclusion and leadership is written with two areas in mind. The first area that is commonly addressed is

---

[3] Matthew W. Brault, "Americans with Disabilities: 2010," *Current Population Reports*, P70–131 (July 2012): 4–13, https://www2.census.gov/library/publications /2012/demo/p70-131.pdf.

[4] David Ranish, "Church Still Has Work to Do with Unreached People Group," *Mission New Network*, March 30, 2011, https://www.mnnonline.org /news/church-still-has-work-to-do-with-unreached-people-group/.

educational inclusion. Studies of this variety often emphasize disability inclusion as it relates to the classroom. As such, the focus tends to be on practices or strategies of inclusion that will enable a person with disabilities to successfully navigate the content of the class in a meaningful and productive manner. Additionally, most inclusive education is attempted in public schools rather than Christian schools. Leadership at Christian schools may have the desire to implement inclusive education, however, they often lack the funding needed to support a viable program for inclusive education. Consequently, the strategies and practices, as well as the environment, present an adaptive hurdle for the church leader.

The second area that is frequently targeted for inclusion studies is corporate leadership. Approaches derived from this type of study often focus on diversity across geography, gender, and generation. The hope of this type of study is to create a business environment where the leader or a leadership team is well represented in each of these three areas. Thus, inclusion is a corporate tactic designed to craft a diverse leadership team for the benefit of business acumen.

It would be a mistake to assume that inclusive studies related to education and corporation would generate little by way of useful information for church ministry. Research in each of these areas can contribute ideas, principles, methods, and skills that could be adapted to address the current need for disability concern within the church. Properly evaluated and adapted, these conclusions can provide the framework for encouraging pastors to become disability-inclusive in their leadership and the church's ministry.

Fourth, the existing literature on disabilities and the Scriptures seems to be presented in two categories that is often at the far ends of the theological spectrum. The voices on the left write along the lines of a social gospel. These authors stress the meeting of needs without a thorough investigation of practical theology. Thus, attention is given to programs or specific ministries but little time is focused on either a theological foundation or evangelistic concerns. Those speaking to the issue from the right predominantly address theological issues while failing to integrate practical components into their theology. Consequently, there is a void of literature that helps church leadership establish and occupy a middle ground that speaks to both their held theology and the implementation of a ministerial component for the disabled.

Each of these four reasons will be central to the purpose of this study. As we look at selected healing episodes in the Gospels, we will examine how Jesus interacted with those who were disabled and consider the inclusive nature of his leadership. As leadership studies delve further into the topic of inclusive leadership, this study will help navigate this terrain from a ministry perspective. Additionally, I will propose ways in which church leadership can model this type of ministry today. In doing so, I will suggest that an inclusive church leader is ultimately a disability-inclusive leader.

Connecting the Biblical Text to Church Leadership

What makes a study like this unique? A number of ministry-related books present approaches and ideas for disability ministry that are loosely connected to select passages of Scripture. However, few resources survey the Scriptures primarily to discover a proper biblical foundation for disability-inclusive leadership in the church.

Some of the earliest literature discussing disability and Scripture is limited to issues related to illness, disease, and medical concerns. Few books address church leadership and disability, or the role a faith community can play in the care of and ministry with the disabled. Rebecca Raphael believes that the newness of disability studies is causing interest in the topic, as well as growth in this research area. She states that earlier studies were predominantly focused on medical perspectives instead of sociocultural assessments or theological perspectives. Raphael identifies Hector Avalos's 1995 monograph titled *Illness and Healthcare in the Ancient Near East* as the first true research related to both the cultural impact of disability and a biblically based response.[5]

---

[5] Rebecca Raphael, *Biblical Corpora: Representations of Disability in Hebrew Biblical Literature* (New York: T&T Clark, 2008), 15–16.

Linguistics also pose a challenge in working with the biblical text as it relates to the modern understanding of disabilities. The lack of a large-scale categorization in Scripture makes it difficult to understand disability in terms of a single word or a specific category. Raphael contends that biblical Hebrew does not have one term that functions as a means of defining or grouping together physical, emotional, and cognitive impairments in the way our word *disabled* is used today. While various impairments like "blind" or "lame" were grouped together, they were not categorized by a single word like modern culture does with the use of the term *disability*.[6]

A biblically thorough study in disabilities requires that scholars cobble together a list of the various ailments described in the Scriptures. Then, with this list gathered, they must study the historical context to see how these ailments might translate into our current understanding of disabilities. A good example of this difficulty might be the woman with the twelve-year blood issue (Matt 9:18–26; Mark 5:21–43; Luke 8:40–56). At some level, we could argue that today, given modern medicine, she would be properly diagnosed and promptly and successfully treated. Thus, her story might not be a disability-related story. However, if we understand the physical, emotional, financial, and spiritual consequences of how an unhealable condition still has current disability implications, we find that her story easily fits the framework of a disability story.

In the book *Copious Hosting*, Jennie Weiss Block uses a Scripture-centric understanding of disabilities (rather than a modern approach). As a result, she is left with a narrow group of texts to study. Block separates illness and disability passages in the Gospels. Further, she separates passages related to Jesus's actions of curing and Jesus's actions of healing. These delimitations, as they relate to the Bible and disability, lead to a critique of three healing passages and a detailed examination of one healing account from the Gospels.[7]

---

[6] Raphael, 14–15.

[7] Jennie Weiss Block, *Copious Hosting: A Theology of Access for People with Disabilities* (New York: Continuum, 2002), 101–13.

To date, there is an insufficient amount of material that connects the biblical record to leadership, practical ministry, and disability concerns. The issues identified in this section may well be the cause for this lack of material. However, I am hopeful that this study will take steps in filling this void in the available academic and practical ministry literature.

Selecting the Texts

This book will focus on leadership matters related to the concern for, and care of, the disabled as taught in Scripture. To accomplish this task, various healing miracles of Jesus will be considered. These miracles will serve as the biblical foundation for disability-inclusive leadership.

Scholars disagree regarding the number of miracles performed by Jesus. Harold L. Willmington identifies thirty-six miracles of Jesus Christ that are recorded in the Gospels. He has separated these miracles into seven different categories.[8] Gaylen Leverett acknowledges thirty-three miracles of Jesus. However, his list generalizes certain miracles thus minimizing the total number of miracles. An example of this generalization is the miraculous catch of fish recorded in Luke 5 and John 21. The miraculous catch of fish in Luke happens at the beginning of Jesus's earthly ministry. John records another miraculous catch of fish that happened toward the end of Jesus's earthly ministry. These two separate events are combined in Leverett's list of Jesus's miracles.[9] Neil S. Wilson and Linda K. Taylor count thirty-five miracles attributed to Jesus Christ. However, they do not separate them into any specific categories or types.[10] House also recognizes thirty-five miracles that he has divided into the two categories

---

[8] Harold L. Willmington, *Willmington's Guide to the Bible* (Wheaton, IL: Tyndale, 1988), 339–40.

[9] Gaylen Leverett, "Matthew: The Kingdom of Heaven," in *The Essence of the New Testament: A Survey*, ed. Elmer Towns and Ben Gutierrez (Nashville: B&H Academic, 2012), 57–58.

[10] Neil S. Wilson and Linda K. Taylor, *Tyndale Handbook of Bible Charts & Maps*, The Tyndale Reference Library (Wheaton, IL: Tyndale House, 2001), 356.

of nature miracles and healing miracles. For H. Wayne House, an event such as the turning of water into wine (John 2:1–11) is classified as a nature miracle while the raising of Lazarus (John 11:1–45) is an example of a healing miracle.[11]

Using House's list of healing miracles as the groundwork for this study, I will concentrate on healing events that are directly connected to disability. Thus, episodes such as the removal of a fever from Peter's mother-in-law (Matt 8:14–15; Mark 1:29–31; Luke 4:38–41) will not be considered. One exception is the healing of Jairus's daughter. This story will be considered because the literary device of interchange or intercalation is used by all three writers. This intercalation, or story within a story, requires the reader to consider how both stories compare and contrast to understand what is being communicated in the text.

To fully discuss particular healing miracles, the selected texts will only include the healing accounts that are included in all three Synoptic Gospels. This allows for the greatest amount of material available for the survey of each healing episode. There are also two healing episodes recorded in the Gospel of John that meet the criteria of a healing performed by Jesus that addresses a disability. These two episodes will also be considered.

Given these parameters, the following healing stories will be used as the basis for this study:

- Curing of the leper near Gennesaret (Matt 8:1–4; Mark 1:40–45; Luke 5:12–15)
- Restoring the paralytic at Capernaum (Matt 9:1–8; Mark 2:1–12; Luke 5:17–26)
- Restoring of the man with the withered hand (Matt 12:9–14; Mark 3:1–6; Luke 6:6–11)
- Curing of the woman with twelve–year bleeding and healing of Jairus's daughter (Matt 9:18–26; Mark 5:21–43; Luke 8:40–56)

---

[11] H. Wayne House, *Chronological and Background Charts of the New Testament*, 2nd ed., Zondervan Charts (Grand Rapids: Zondervan Academic, 2009), 112–15.

- Restoring sight to blind Bartimaeus (Matt 20:29–34; Mark 10:46–52; Luke 18:35–43)
- Healing of the lame man at Bethesda (John 5:1–17)
- Healing of the man born blind (John 9–10:21)

The Synoptic Gospels record two accounts of demon possession. One deals with a boy who had multiple medical issues that Jesus addressed while rebuking an evil spirit (Matt 17:14–19; Mark 9:14–29; Luke 9:37–43). At face value this story meets the considerations for this study. However, this narrative will not be examined due to the complexity of the elements in the story as well as its connection to the supernatural. Indeed, it is the element of the supernatural that marks this story out as different from all of the healing accounts considered here.

Inclusive Leadership: Starting Points

As the number of people with disabilities increases, more studies are being conducted on inclusive leadership as it relates to leaders who have a disability. Studies of this nature attempt to demonstrate that much can be learned by employing a person with a disability in an upper management position. Much wisdom on disability-inclusive leadership can be gained from studying inclusion as it relates to employing a person with disabilities in a leadership position. This will not be the focus of this book. Rather, it will address leadership characteristics that approach disabilities in a manner that promotes inclusion within the church. While it is true that an end result of disability-inclusive leadership should lead to the employment of people with disabilities in viable leadership positions, this goal is not the emphasis of this book.

Further, studies in inclusive leadership can also take the shape of team building or creating a diverse leadership staff. While there is certainly value in examining inclusive leadership through such a lens, it is incongruent to the ministry Jesus shared with his disciples. These disciples were followers of Jesus and not team members, or even colleagues. While Jesus did address his disciples as friends (John 15:15), Scripture indicates that the relationship Jesus had with his disciples was not one of equal significance.

Instead, the focus of this study is singularly directed to compassion and inclusion for the disabled. To that end, there are several terms that routinely show up in discussion related to leadership, disability, and inclusion. To ensure that we are all on the same page, I would like to give some consideration to these terms before moving forward.

At the heart of this study is the belief that those who are disabled should be involved in the full body life of the church. A proper understanding of a disability-inclusive church will show that inclusion is built on the foundation "that all individuals with disabilities have a right to be included in naturally occurring settings and activities with their neighborhood peers, siblings, and friends."[12] Thus, those who are disabled will find opportunities to be involved in the local church. Pastors and church leaders who pursue disability inclusion in the church will not be content with an attend, sit, listen, leave approach to disability ministry.

There seems to be no end to the writing of books on leadership. Indeed, this book represents one more title that seeks to explore what it means to be a leader within the context of the church. While the lens used in this book for examining church leadership is unique, the definition of church leadership employed here certainly is not. As Henry T. Blackaby and Richard Blackaby noted, leadership is "Moving people on to God's agenda."[13] For disability-inclusive leadership, this means that pastors, church leadership, and the congregation begin to see compassion for, care of, and inclusion of the disabled as something God desires. Consequently, compassion, care, and inclusion become a desire of pastors, church leadership, and the congregation as well.

The term *inclusive leadership* is variously understood. For some, inclusive leadership involves a senior management team that includes a team member

---

[12] E. J. Erwin, "The Philosophy and Status of Inclusion," *Envision: A Publication of Lighthouse National Center for Vision and Child Development* 1 (1993): 1.

[13] Henry T. Blackaby and Richard Blackaby, *Spiritual Leadership: Moving People on to God's Agenda* (Nashville: B&H, 2001), 20.

who is disabled. Thus, employees might say, "Our executive administration is a model of inclusive leadership." Similarly, inclusive leadership can be represented by a leadership team that encompasses diversity in gender, geography, and generation.

While the above examples of inclusion at the group level are correct, they do not address the topic of inclusive leadership at the personal level. What makes an individual inclusive in their approach to leadership? Inclusive leadership at the level of the individual can best be summarized as "Leaders who exhibit openness, accessibility and availability in their interactions with followers."[14] Pastors and church leaders who model these three relational qualities create an atmosphere where congregations can grow in both their understanding of disability as well as their desire to be involved in the lives of those who are disabled. In turn, this community of faith becomes a place of welcome for those who have a disability. Inclusive leadership, as it relates to disabilities, is a character trait that expands beyond the leader to the community so that those involved in the group share a similar attitude toward disability.

When these terms are taken together, a picture of a disability leadership begins to develop. Disability-inclusive leadership is a type of leadership characterized by an awareness of those with disabilities and a desire to include those with disabilities. For the pastor and church leader, disability-inclusive leadership is rooted in Scripture and modeled by Jesus through his interaction with those who are disabled. This approach to leadership spills over to others so that those within a pastor's circle of influence find themselves desiring to be disability-inclusive leaders as well.

Perhaps the best treatment of inclusive leadership from a Christian perspective comes from Steve Echols. In an article entitled "Transformational/ Servant Leadership: A Potential Synergism for an Inclusive Leadership Style,"

---

[14] Abraham Carmeli, Roni Reiter-Palmon, and Enbal Ziv, "Inclusive Leadership and Employee Involvement in Creative Tasks in the Workplace: The Mediating Role of Psychological Safety," *Creativity Research Journal* 22, no. 3 (August 12, 2010): 4, https://doi.org/10.1080/10400419.2010.504654.

Echols lays the groundwork for understanding inclusive leadership as an appropriate blend of transformational leadership and servant leadership. At the intersection of these two leadership styles are the purpose and approach of the church. Echols argues that "transformational leadership is the mission of the church and servant leadership is the mode."[15]

With this crossroads in mind, Echols believes there are five characteristics of an inclusive leader who has learned the blend and balance of transformational leadership and servant leadership. Echols proposes that inclusive leadership has the following characteristics.

First, inclusive leadership brings the maximum number of individuals into participation. . . . Second, inclusive leadership empowers individuals to reach their full potential while pursuing the common good of the particular populace. . . . Third, those who practice inclusive leadership develop a culture that perpetuates the morality of the worth of the individual in such a way as to act as a preventive resistance against the ever-present possibility of despotism. . . . Fourth, inclusive leadership is intentional in the replication of today's leaders who model the above characteristics with a commitment to allow future leadership to emerge. . . . Finally, inclusive leadership is manifested in the development of appropriate boundaries that maintain the integrity of the nature of the collective without marginalizing any of the populace.[16]

In this book, I will use these five characteristics as the grid to evaluate and demonstrate the inclusive nature of Jesus's ministry to the disabled. Indeed, I believe that the selected healing miracles that are surveyed in this book will show that Jesus modeled inclusive leadership as Echols understands it. Thus, pastors and church leaders can model the inclusive leadership of Jesus Christ through disability-inclusive leadership.

---

[15] Steve Echols, "Transformational/Servant Leadership: A Potential Synergism for an Inclusive Leadership Style," *Journal of Religious Leadership* 8, no. 2 (2009): 115.

[16] Echols, 88–91.

2

Jesus and the Disabled in the Synoptic Gospels

A newly engaged couple is shopping for wedding rings. They are looking for something special that captures their hearts and imaginations. One of their friends asks them if they know what type of rings they want. Exchanging glances at each other, they respond by saying, "We'll know it when we see it." Four years later, the couple has decided to move out of their rented apartment and into their first home. As they meet with the real estate agent, she asks them if they know what they want in their first house. They list a few of their must-haves and non-negotiables. They also reveal to her their budget and some of their dream amenities. The agent smiles and says that the market is competitive. They will need to make a decision quickly when they find something they like. The couple looks at each other with that familiar look and agrees that making a decision will not be that complicated. Almost in unison, they respond to the real estate agent, "We'll know it when we see it."

There are, of course, many other times in life that such an expression fits perfectly. The same is true for examining characteristics and qualities in Scripture. Often one ends up reading a biblical text and recognizing a trait or type within the pages of Holy Writ. With this possibility in mind, can we go to God's Word and ask, "Is there something inherently obvious about the ministry of Jesus as it pertains to inclusion?" More specifically, as one examines Jesus's interaction with the disabled, is it possible to discern character traits of inclusive leadership?

To discern these character traits, we must have an idea of how to go about studying the Scriptures. This means we need to be able to conduct a study of Scripture that moves from broad categories to narrow ones. More specifically, we need to be able to move from studying the Scriptures in general to studying the narratives found in the Gospels and finally to a specific kind of narrative—the miracle stories. A proper exegesis of Scripture will recognize the literary uniqueness of the various genres and subgenres found on the pages of the Bible.

Studying the Scriptures

Examining the stories of Scripture comes with its own set of challenges. The most basic of these challenges is a commitment to faithfulness. Lindsay Olesberg recognizes that there is a dual nature to faithfulness when studying the narratives of Scripture. She believes that we must have a faithfulness to the individual story, as well as a faithfulness to the grand story, or metanarrative, of Scripture. A true study of the stories of the Scriptures will keep in mind how they fit into the all-encompassing story of God's work in his world.[1] Olesberg's dual challenges are worth noting in any study of the Scriptures; however, they are of primary importance to this study for two reasons. First, they serve as a word of caution. While each story is studied as an individual narrative, it cannot be at the expense of the full redemptive

---

[1] Lindsay Olesberg, *The Bible Study Handbook: A Comprehensive Guide to an Essential Practice* (Downers Grove, IL: InterVarsity, 2012), 101.

narrative of Scripture. Second, the goal of this study is to understand the ways Jesus's ministry was inclusive in nature. If the stories of Jesus's ministry are inclusive, then it stands to reason that the message of Scripture—the one story that every story is telling—is an inclusive one as well.

Richard Alan Fuhr and Andreas J. Köstenberger, borrowing from Roy Zuck in *Basic Bible Interpretation*, acknowledge that there are three distinct challenges for any study of Scripture. These challenges can be categorized as historical, literary, and theological. Each of these challenges includes distinctive gaps that highlight the difficulty presented in each category. To study the historical context of a text of the Bible, one must recognize gaps of time, geography, and culture. Each of these gaps reflect the understanding that modern society is far removed from the era, location, and civilization represented in the biblical stories. Examining the literary component of the Scriptures requires an acknowledgment of both the language and literary gap between the events of the Bible and present-day culture. These two gaps emphasize the differences in language and literature that recount the numerous events found in God's Word. Finally, the theological challenge is underscored by the supernatural gap, the theological gap, and the appropriation gap. In the supernatural gap, one admits that certain events of Scripture are not things that are commonly experienced in the natural world. The theological gap addresses the reality that the Scriptures are God's self-revelation and should be approached with the understanding of the truth he is communicating in and through it. An appropriation gap highlights the challenge of moving from interpretation to application when it comes to the study of the Scriptures. It is not enough to simply interpret the Scriptures. Rather, a successful examination of a passage of God's Word will move from interpretation to proper and appropriate application of the commands, examples, instructions, and exhortations found in the examined biblical text.[2]

---

[2] Richard Alan Fuhr and Andreas J. Köstenberger, *Inductive Bible Study: Observation, Interpretation, and Application Through the Lenses of History, Literature, and Theology* (Nashville: B&H Academic, 2016), 4–19.

The three challenges presented by Fuhr and Köstenberger are crucial to recognize in this study of Scripture. Of preeminent importance to this study on Jesus's encounter with the disabled are the culture, time, literary, supernatural, theological, and appropriation gaps. While the other gaps pose a certain level of significance, their importance is diminished due to the more literary and less exegetical study undertaken here. Where issues related to the likes of language or geography are presented as central to interpretation, they will be considered. However, since this is not a verse-by-verse exegetical study, these types of gaps will not be intentionally pursued.

Studying the Gospels

Among the various genres of Scripture are the narrative stories of the Old and New Testaments. Robert H. Stein alleges that this is the literary form that dominates the Bible. According to his calculations, over 40 percent of the Old Testament and nearly 60 percent of the New Testament is written in narrative form. He notes popular books like Genesis, Exodus, Joshua, Esther, and large parts of Numbers, Deuteronomy, and the Prophets as being narrative in literary form. In the New Testament, the books of Matthew, Mark, Luke, John, and Acts are written as narrative. The predominance of this type of literature leads Stein to conclude that, for most people, their first encounter with the Bible is through the avenue of a narrative.[3]

If Stein's calculations are true, there must be a method to studying the stories of the Scripture that keeps in step with a faithful understanding of the individual story and the grand redemptive story that ties all the stories together. This method of study would recognize the literary form of narrative as well as honor the theological focus of Scripture when studying the stories of the Bible. To study the narratives of the Bible without either of these considerations would be to do injustice to the story and the divine author of the story.

---

[3] Robert H. Stein, *A Basic Guide to Interpreting the Bible: Playing by the Rules*, 2nd ed. (Grand Rapids: Baker, 2011), 79.

Leland Ryken suggests that to analyze the characters in a biblical narrative in general, or the Gospels in particular, one should first assemble the cast of characters in the story. Next, the reader should determine which character is the protagonist, which character is the antagonist, and what other characters play a minor role in the function of the story. When considering the major characters, Ryken suggests that the reader assemble a list of important details like traits, roles, relationships, and external as well as internal actions. Additionally, one should be able reach some conclusions about the characters in the story based on their lives. These conclusions culminate in the understanding of the kind of example put forward by the characters of the story. Do the major characters represent a good example to follow or a bad example to avoid? For Ryken, every story is an example story at some level.[4]

J. Scott Duvall and J. Daniel Hays argue that the Gospels are a Christological biography that focuses on Jesus's life and teaching. For readers to correctly understand the stories that make up the Gospels, they must grasp the two specific purposes behind each of the four Gospels. First, through the leading of the Holy Spirit, the authors of the Gospels have both selected and arranged the content to tell the story of Jesus Christ. Second, the authors are using story as a means of communicating something to their first readers. To properly understand these stories, one must understand what the author is saying to them and to us.[5]

Ryken proposes that these stories within the Gospels be treated as biographical stories. He attributes this understanding to the documentary approach that is employed to record these events in the life of Jesus Christ. As such, what the reader experiences is the showing and telling of what happened, rather than how it happened. Ryken suggests that a proper study of

---

[4] Leland Ryken, *Jesus the Hero: A Guided Literary Study of the Gospels*, Reading the Bible as Literature (Wooster, OH: Weaver, 2016), 28–29.

[5] J. Scott Duvall and J. Daniel Hays, *Grasping God's Word: A Hands-On Approach to Reading, Interpreting, and Applying the Bible*, 3rd ed. (Grand Rapids: Zondervan Academic, 2012), 273.

these passages will focus on the following: what Jesus says or does, what role or roles Jesus fills, how others respond to Jesus, what conclusions can be reached about the person and work of Jesus based on the material presented in the story, and how the reader should respond to Jesus with regard to belief, allegiance, and behavior.[6]

Ryken's list gives a basic structure for investigating the events of Jesus's life as they are recorded in Scripture. It directs readers to what they should be paying attention to, what is being shown, and what is being told about Jesus. It also cautions against drawing assumptions about how something happened. These biographic or documentary-style stories are not designed to encourage a textual understanding that is rooted in assumptions. Thus, speculation on how something occurred should not be engaged unless it is clearly presented in the text. Ryken's list will serve as the method to gather the specific information that will be examined in each biblical story studied in this survey. Consequently, this study will examine specific passages of Scripture with an eye toward what Jesus is saying or doing, the role that he is playing (primarily as miracle worker or healer), how others in the story are responding to Jesus, and what conclusions the story asks us to make about who Jesus is and what his work on earth is about. Ryken's fifth study question, the question of response, will be used in conjunction with Echols's inclusive leadership framework. Therefore, Ryken's response question will be examined with an eye toward Jesus's structure of inclusive leadership.

Studying the Miracle Stories

Within the genre of the Gospels are a specific type of story identified as miracle stories. Typically, a story where Jesus heals an individual, demonstrates control over the natural world, or reveals his power and authority over the spiritual world is considered a miracle story. Eric Eve describes the miracle stories and biblical miracles as an event that causes surprise because it is considered unimaginable for a human being to accomplish. Thus, God

---

[6] Ryken, *Jesus the Hero*, 36–37.

has acted in either a direct manner or through an intermediary.[7] For Ryken, the miracle stories of Jesus highlight a primary concern in Jesus's years of public ministry. These stories are noted for their variety. This diversity is represented by the way they are told and the meaning they intend to convey. They may shed light on Jesus's divine power or communicate a lesson on faith and obedience.[8]

Negatively, W. Randolph Tate asserts that some critics view the miracle stories of the Gospels as aretalogy (a story where the actions of a divine character are both phenomenal and supernatural). These stories, like other aretalogical stories, highlight Jesus's ability to do supernatural things. As such, the reader is brought to a point of conversion and belief in the person of Jesus Christ as the son of God.[9] While Tate's spotlight on the negative perspective of the miracle stories should be noted, one needs to recognize that Christian historians and theologians regard these stories as historically accurate. This belief stands in direct contrast to the mythological nature of other aretalogical stories.

These three descriptions of the miracle stories, when combined with the understanding that the Gospels are telling something of Jesus through the story itself as well as the selection and arrangement of the story, enlighten an examination of the passages addressed in this study. The stories that will be explored are not simply basic interactions that Jesus had with the average villager or citizen. Rather, these are stories selected and arranged to communicate how God, through Jesus, is responding to those who have been marginalized or excluded in their culture.

Studying the miracle stories of Jesus requires a basis for making vital observations and gathering the necessary information. Having this structure ensures that crucial details are not missed during the studying and recording

---

[7] Eric Eve, *The Jewish Context of Jesus' Miracles (Journal for the Study of the New Testament Supplement*, no. 231) (Sheffield, UK: Sheffield Academic, 2002), 1.

[8] Ryken, *Jesus the Hero*, 56–57.

[9] W. Randolph Tate, *Handbook for Biblical Interpretation: An Essential Guide to Methods, Terms, and Concepts*, 2nd ed. (Grand Rapids: Baker Academic, 2012), 29.

stage. When examining the miracle stories of Jesus, Ryken suggests that the reader pay attention to a typical formula found in most biblical accounts of these divine miracles. First, a need is established. Second, the help of Jesus is sought. Third, either the person in need or one of their acquaintances will convey faith or obedience. Fourth, Jesus performs a miracle related to the need. Finally, the actions of the characters in the story demonstrate a response to the particular miracle and/or Jesus. Ryken notes that one or more of these features may be absent from a particular story. However, they generally follow that observable pattern.[10]

This study of the healing miracles Jesus performed on those with a disability will pay attention to Ryken's miracle story formula while regarding his list of questions for biographical or gospel stories. This combination will provide both the groundwork for study and the tools to unearth the necessary content for making conclusions about Jesus's method of inclusive leadership. As a whole, this formula and these questions will help ensure fidelity both to the stories themselves and to the one story of Scripture. Each of these elements will contribute to the brief synopsis of the healing story that will lead into the study of that particular story as it is recorded in the Synoptic Gospels. This overview will first summarize the story and then focus on the elements that are either similar or different in the three recordings of the miracle.

---

[10] Ryken, *Jesus the Hero*, 56.

(3)

Curing of a Leper
Near Gennesaret

(Matthew 8:1–4; Mark 1:40–45;
Luke 5:12–15)

Jesus had made his way from the mountains down into the town. While he was there, a man with a serious skin disease approached Jesus, fell on his face, and asked to be healed. Moved with emotion, Jesus reached out, touched the man, and healed him. Once the man was healed, he was sternly instructed not to tell anyone. He was also to go to the priest and make the necessary offering. The offering would serve as a testimony to them. However, the man left Jesus's presence and began to tell people what had happened to him. Jesus was no longer able to move through the town freely and had to relocate to deserted places. However, people still came and sought him out.

The three Gospel accounts of this story share numerous similarities. Each writer recounts the serious nature of the man's skin disease. He was a leper (Matt 8:2; Mark 1:40; Luke 5:12). All three writers describe the humble nature assumed by the man in his kneeling before Jesus as he requests healing (Matt 8:2; Mark 1:40; Luke 5:12). Each writer records the initial conversation between the man and Jesus with the same kind of detail (Matt 8:2; Mark 1:40; Luke 5:12). The same is also true about Jesus's spoken response to the man with the skin disease (Matt 8:3; Mark 1:41; Luke 5:13). Further, all three writers mention that Jesus touched the man to perform the healing, and the immediacy of that healing (Matt 8:3; Mark 1:41–42; Luke 5:13). Finally, each writer also identifies that Jesus gave one negative instruction followed by three positive points of instruction (Matt 8:4; Mark 1:43–44; Luke 5:14). Negatively, all three note that the man was instructed not to tell anyone what had occurred. Conversely, each of these three Gospel writers record what the now-cured man should do. He was to go, show himself to the priest, and offer what the Mosaic law would dictate given his circumstance. Once again, all three writers note the reason for these three positive instructions. The actions of this man were to be a testimony to the priest and those who witnessed this presentation (Matt 8:4; Mark 1:44; Luke 5:14).

With this much in common over a story that only spans fourteen verses in three Gospels, one would be tempted to think there are very few differences in the recording of this healing performed by Jesus. Indeed, the similarities outnumber the differences. Yet the differences contribute significant content to properly understanding the story. These differences are most pronounced in Mark's Gospel. It is in this recounting of the event that Jesus's emotion is clearly seen. Mark notes the compassion that moves Jesus (Mark 1:41), as well as the stern nature of Jesus's warning for the man not to tell anyone (Mark 1:43), but to go to the priest, show himself, and offer the necessary gift. Mark also records the now-cured man's inability to follow Jesus's instruction (Mark 1:45). Mark notes that after the man left Jesus, he went out announcing what had just happened to him. Thus, Mark concludes that Jesus was now forced to deserted places, and people would come from many places to see and hear him (Mark 1:45).

Luke concludes his recording of this story by mentioning that information about Jesus spread even more. Thus, large crowds would gather to hear him and to be healed. This pressure led Jesus to withdraw to deserted places to pray (Luke 5:15–16). Taken in connection with Mark's conclusion, it can be understood that the now-cured man's refusal to do as Jesus ordered him led to the news of Jesus spreading even more. Consequently, when Jesus would seek sanctuary in deserted places in order to pray, crowds would pursue him to hear his message and to be healed of their various maladies.

Luke, a physician by trade, was the only writer to provide a description of the man's serious skin condition. He recorded that this man's disease was "all over him" (Luke 5:12), impacting his entire body. Since Luke was a doctor, I believe this shows us his eye for medical detail. For the reader, the information Luke provided helps establish the severity of this man's disability. It was not simply a finger, a hand, an arm, a toe, or a leg that was impacted by this disease, but rather the man's whole body.

Perhaps it is Luke's eye for detail that leads to one other observation that should be noted in Luke's documentation of this healing. Luke provides the most detail on the man's approach to Jesus before he makes his request. It is in Luke that the reader sees a man who does more than just fall to his knees in humility. Rather, Luke writes that he fell facedown before Jesus and begged him for healing on the condition of Jesus's willingness (Luke 5:12). While Mark records the emotion of Jesus. Luke records the emotion of this man with a serious skin disease.

Each component of Ryken's miracle story structure is present in this account. This narrative presents the story of a man with a most serious plight. A need is clearly established. This man was a leper. Yet he was also a humble man who knew that Jesus could heal him. So he sought Jesus's help and expressed his faith by acknowledging the possibility for healing at the discretion of Jesus Christ. Jesus performed a miracle by touching the leper and healing him. While Jesus commanded a specific response from the man, what is in view is a man who did the opposite and proclaimed his healing so widely that the news about Jesus spread.

To better comprehend how this story addresses the inclusive nature of Jesus's ministry, three components of this passage merit further examination. First, one needs a better grasp of the man's serious skin disease or leprosy. Second, an evaluation of Jesus's emotive reaction as recorded by Mark needs to be undertaken. Finally, the significance of Jesus's healing through touch ought to be pursued.

The Serious Skin Disease

Understanding the biblical disease known as leprosy presents a cultural challenge. Is it proper to assume that our modern medical diagnosis of leprosy is consistent with the way the Scriptures present this disease? Stanley G. Browne states that one cannot be certain that the current condition known as Hansen's disease is the equivalent to leprosy in the Bible. This uncertainty is primarily the result of early Hippocratic use of the word *lepra* to describe any scaly, desquamating skin condition with no indication that the disease included what is currently described as leprosy.[1] Jeffrey John identifies leprosy as a catchall word that described a number of skin conditions in the Bible. As such, he believes it does not necessarily refer to the "dreadful, wasting, muscular, and skin disease for which the word is used today."[2] Tomohiro Omiya asserts that there is a general consensus amongst scholars that the skin disease identified as leprosy in the Bible is not akin to a Hansen's disease diagnosis today. Further, it is probably not associated with other current specific skin diseases. According to Omiya, the best way to understand the biblical use of the word *leprosy* is to recognize that it is a serious skin disease.[3]

---

[1] Stanley G. Browne and Christian Medical Fellowship, *Leprosy in the Bible* (London: Christian Medical Fellowship, 1979), 22.

[2] Jeffrey John, *The Meaning in the Miracles* (Grand Rapids: Eerdmans, 2004), 26.

[3] Tomohiro Omiya, "Leprosy," in *Dictionary of Jesus and the Gospels,* 2nd ed., ed. Joel B. Green (Downers Grove, IL: IVP Academic, 2013), 517.

While one may not be able to identify leprosy with any specific contemporary disease or skin condition, one can identify the impact of contracting this skin disease during biblical times. Leviticus 13:1–14:57 describes the purification rituals for various skin diseases that infect human beings, clothing, and whole houses. Mark Rooker acknowledges that the terminology used to describe the skin diseases discussed in these two chapters is quite general and covers things from mildew to leprosy.[4] What should not be missed in these two chapters, according to Omiya, is that they designate anyone or anything that contracts this serious skin disease as unclean in keeping with the parameters established by Jewish law. These two chapters address the need for all things designated as unclean to be removed from God's community.[5] Thus, Omiya suggests that the emphasis here is not on medical instructions for treating skin disease but purity rituals for maintaining cleanliness within Israel.[6] John Pilch identifies leprosy, as it is to be understood in the Bible, not with a certain medical diagnosis but with the social stigma it created. Leprosy threatened the wholeness and integrity of God's community. Consequently, it was necessary to remove those who had contracted it from the community.[7] With this understanding in mind, Jeffrey John addresses the grim reality a leper would experience during biblical times:

> The leper was an object of horror in Jesus's society, not only because of the terror of the disease itself, but also because it rendered the sufferer ritually unclean—non-kosher. A leper was to be excluded both from corporate worship and from all social interaction, since not only was the disease regarded as physically contagious, but the ritual uncleanness it caused also was regarded as contaminating.

---

[4] Mark F. Rooker, *Leviticus*, New American Commentary, vol. 3a (Nashville: B&H, 2000), 90.

[5] Omiya, "Leprosy," 517.

[6] Omiya, 517.

[7] John Pilch, "Healing in Mark: A Social Science Analysis," *Biblical Theological Bulletin* 15, no. 4 (1985): 142–50.

Anyone the leper touched would have been similarly excluded from public worship and from all social intercourse until examined and declared clean by the priest. Exhaustive rules concerning the quarantining of lepers are laid down in Leviticus, one of which was that if anyone approached, they were to shout "Unclean! Unclean!"[8]

The leper in this miracle story forwent the required pronouncement and, prostrate before Jesus, pled for healing. Since Matthew, by way of introducing this story, records that large crowds followed Jesus, and Luke notes that Jesus was in a town when this confrontation took place, the actions of this man jeopardized the cleanliness of more than just himself and Jesus. This act is one of desperation by a man whose plight has left him a societal outcast. However, Jesus also reacts in a manner uncommon for the treatment of the leprous. Rather than only speaking a word of healing, Jesus touches the man and pronounces his healing. Jeffrey John affirms this understanding of the passage by recognizing that the leper breaks Levitical rules by approaching Jesus. His shocking behavior expresses both his desperation and his faith. In turn, Jesus's response to this man's rule-breaking is an even greater display of rule-breaking. Jesus does the unthinkable by touching the leper. Instead of the disease transferring from the man to Jesus, healing flows from Jesus to this man.[9]

The Emotion of Jesus

Mark's recording of the emotion expressed by Jesus provides another glimpse into his view on disability. It is only in Mark's Gospel that Jesus is described as being moved with compassion before he healed the leper. Mark is also the only writer to record the stern warning given by Jesus to the man as he dismissed him from his presence. At the heart of the first of these emotive

---

[8] John, *Meaning in the Miracles*, 26–27.
[9] John, 27–28.

displays is a textual difficulty that may be clarified by the second accounting of Jesus's emotion.

At face value, there appears to be very little to discuss with regard to the compassion Jesus felt when he encountered the leper in Mark 1:41. Most of our modern translations use words that express similarity in how Jesus felt during this encounter. The New Living Translation (NLT), New American Standard Bible (NASB), King James Bible (KJV), New King James Bible (NKJV), and the Christian Standard Bible (CSB) all identify Jesus as being "moved with compassion." Further, the English Standard Version (ESV) identifies Jesus as being "moved with pity." However, one modern translation proposes something that appears to disagree with each of these translations. The New International Version (NIV) states "Jesus was indignant." What lies behind this translation difference and does it tell us something about Jesus's perspective on disability?

Greek professor and committee member for the New International Version, Bill Mounce notes that the issue is related to a variation in the Greek texts. Mounce maintains that the NIV follows the reading of *orgistheis* ("to make angry"), while the other translations choose to follow the reading *splanchnistheis* ("to be moved with pity, or compassion"). Externally, *orgistheis* is read by Codex Bezae (D), and a few Latin manuscripts (a ff2 r1*). While *splanchnistheis* is read by ℵ B D it sa(mss) bo(pt) and others. Mounce concludes that there is "very little question here that the external eviden[ce] supports σπλαγχνισθείς [*splanchnistheis*]." He acknowledges that neither Matt 8:3 nor Luke 5:13 include either word, thus strengthening the external evidence. As to the NIV, Mounce contends that the translation choice is based on internal evidence. He believes it is more likely that the harder reading of *orgistheis* is the changed version. Thus, while it may seem odd to imagine, Jesus becomes indignant or "angry" when the leper proclaims that Jesus is able to heal him but lacks the confidence that Jesus would want to perform this healing miracle. For Mounce, this type of explanation would make sense if one considers that this story takes place very early on in Jesus's ministry and at a time when he is a relatively unknown quantity. Thus, he concludes that it is more likely that a scribe softened *orgistheis* to *splanchnistheis*.[10]

David E. Garland, in the NIV Application Commentary on Mark, believes that *orgistheis* may be the original reading. If this is the case, Jesus is not annoyed at the leper for breeching ritual protocol. Rather, he is expressing the anger of God toward the devastation this serious skin disease causes. For Garland, this anger is matched by compassion in the purposeful touch of Jesus in performing this healing. This human contact by a "clean" individual was perhaps the first time the leper had felt human contact in quite some time.[11]

Robert A. Guelich argues that choosing *orgistheis* over *splanchnistheis* means choosing the more difficult reading over the better attested one and creates the problem of Jesus's anger. As a resolution to this difficulty, he notes that some scholars see Jesus as a miracle worker whose power is stirring within him. As such, there is an agitation when he is confronted by this physical need. Guelich remains unconvinced by their arguments. Instead, he places Jesus's anger as being directed at the "distortion of God's creature by the forces of evil." Jesus's anger is a righteous anger at the work of the Evil One in those who are sick.[12]

Addressing this textual variance, James R. Edwards notes that Jesus's anger in this situation seems wrong. The shock of an angry Jesus might argue for the originality of this reading. Yet Edwards asserts that copyists had a tendency to change readings that were difficult to ones that were more acceptable. Since both Matthew and Luke do not specifically identify the sentiment expressed by Jesus in this event, it is conceivable that Jesus's emotion was one of anger rather than compassion. Edwards believes that, like God's anger at the affliction experienced by Israel in Judg 10:16, Jesus's

---

[10] Bill Mounce, "A Little Text Criticism (Mark 1:41)," March 24, 2013, https://billmounce.com/blog/little-text-criticism-mark-1-41.

[11] David E. Garland, *Mark*, NIV Application Commentary (Grand Rapids: Zondervan Academic, 1996), 75–76.

[12] Robert A. Guelich, *Mark 1–8:26*, Word Biblical Commentary, vol. 34a (Waco, TX: Word Books, 1989), 74.

anger is directed toward the misery this leper faced. Jesus's healing of this leper is performed in holy wrath so that he was immediately healed of his leprosy.[13]

While the majority of current translations have chosen the easier reading of "compassion" over the harder reading of "anger," further internal evidence points to the harder reading of anger. Edwards identifies Jesus's instructions to the now-clean leper as abrupt and adamant. Specifically, he contends:

> The word for "strong warning" is literally "snorting" in Greek, deriving from the Hebrew word for anger (*'ap*), meaning "to flare the nostrils." The word for "send away" is likewise stronger in Greek than in the NIV. Often used for expelling demons, the expression (Gk. *ekballein*) means that Jesus sent him packing.[14]

This strength and immediacy of Jesus's instruction is also affirmed by Guelich. In his commentary on this passage, Guelich understands the expression of Jesus's stern or strong warning as "silenced him." He notes that this verb expresses a robust emotional reaction that, when used in other New Testament passages, underscores displeasure or anger.[15] France notes that "sternly warned" should be understood as "strictly charged" rather than something like "scolding" or worse. However, he also recognizes that a note of anger must be acknowledged in the understanding of Jesus's warning to the healed man since other similar uses of this word in the Old Testament communicate this type of emotion.[16] Brooks also emphasizes the emotive nature to Jesus's warning and dismissal of the once-diseased man. He notes that "with strong warning" highlights strong inner-personal feelings and could also be translated as "to be angry," "to scold," and "to warn." Additionally, the verb translated "sent away," also used in Mark 1:43, typically means

---

[13] James R. Edwards, *The Gospel According to Mark*, Pillar New Testament Commentary (Grand Rapids: Eerdmans, 2002), 70.

[14] Edwards, 70.

[15] Guelich, *Mark 1–8:26*, 74. See also Matt 9:30; Mark 14:5; John 11:33, 38.

[16] R. T. France, *The Gospel of Mark*, New International Greek Testament Commentary (Grand Rapids: Eerdmans, 2002), 119.

"to cast out." Often, it is used in conjunction with the expelling of demons as it is in Mark 1:34, 39.[17]

Once again, Mark gives the reader a glimpse at the humanity of Jesus through the display of emotion. Jesus expressed notable and pronounced passion that the healed man quickly leave and tell no one of what happened. As presented earlier, Jesus was abrupt and adamant. He had clearly and forcefully communicated what he expected from this man now that he has been healed.

Taken together, the anger of Jesus combined with his stern warning, helps clarify the general feeling of Jesus's emotion that Mark communicates in this narrative. His anger was not directed at the man for his failure to follow the required protocols and thus jeopardize the cleanliness of himself, his disciples, and the crowd that followed him. Neither was Jesus angry that this man believed he could help him but did not think that he would want to heal him. Instead, Jesus's anger was directed to the way that leprosy had impacted the physical and social condition of God's created world. This man, created in the image of God, was physically marred by a serious skin disease that left him marginalized and excluded from all religious and social interaction. If it is not good for human beings to be alone (Gen 2:18), then this man's forlorn condition is the kind of thing that would cause Jesus to express deep emotion. This passion results in the messianic and miracle-worker action that upends loneliness and restores fellowship and community.

The Touch of Jesus

In this healing story, one encounters a man who was living a desolate and despondent life, devoid of any human contact. Then, he experienced the healing touch of Jesus, and that touch was the catalyst for restoration in his life.

---

[17] James A. Brooks, *Mark*, New American Commentary, vol. 23 (Nashville: Broadman, 1991), 56.

William Hendriksen observes that in numerous places the Gospels record the healing touch of Jesus. Sometimes this healing came from Jesus touching the individual, and at other times this healing occurred when the individual touched Jesus. However, Hendriksen carefully notes that healing did not occur because the touch of Jesus had a magical quality about it. Instead, healing took place because it poured out of the divine and human heart beating within Jesus. There was healing in the touch of Jesus because he was and still is, "touched with the feeling of our infirmities" (Heb 4:15 KJV).[18]

In *The Meaning in the Miracles*, Jeffrey John also addresses the significance of touch in this miracle story of healing. He points out that readers see in Jesus's action a demonstration of his desire "to touch the untouchable and embrace the rejected in the new kingdom he proclaims."[19] John stresses that this healing is the first in many of Jesus's encounters with the marginalized. While these people were excluded by society, they are included by Jesus. Their inclusion is demonstrated by Jesus's healing of them and the manner in which he engages them. Thus, individuals like lepers, tax collectors, Gentiles, prostitutes, adulterers, Samaritans, those with physical disabilities, and a woman with a menstrual issue were all included by Jesus. These were certainly not the kinds of people with whom other rabbis associated. Indeed, they would deem them untouchable. However, these were the very kinds of people who were openly accepted in the new kingdom.[20]

Graham Twelftree indicates a threefold importance to Jesus touching the leper to heal him. In touching the leper, the witness of Jesus's life shares the same resemblance to the spoken message of his life. Jesus did not come to break the law. However, in his teaching and in his life, he reveals the divine intention in the law and of his healing. Second, Jesus's touching of the leper draws attention to his desire to be associated with those who were socially and ceremonially considered societal outcasts. Finally, in touching

---

[18] William Hendriksen, *Exposition of the Gospel According to Mark*, Baker New Testament Commentary (Grand Rapids: Baker, 1975), 79.

[19] John, *Meaning in the Miracles*, 30.

[20] John, 29–30.

the leper, Jesus demonstrates his power over leprosy. Instead of Jesus being contaminated by touch, the leper is healed by that same touch.[21]

To the onlookers in the crowds that followed Jesus, there is shock in a leper approaching Jesus rather than retreating and announcing, "Unclean! Unclean!" This shock is met by an even greater astonishment when Jesus reaches out and touches the man to heal him. Jesus is unmistakably demonstrating that those who find themselves marginalized and cast out of the religious and social sector of his day were welcomed in his new kingdom. Indeed, the touch of Jesus applied to this leper proclaims that this kingdom is one of healing and inclusion regardless of physical infirmity. However, one difference marks this story of healing and inclusion for the modern reader. While this healed leper was charged to keep this miraculous healing silent, today believers are commanded to go into all the world and announce the coming of this new and inclusive kingdom of God.

---

[21] Graham H. Twelftree, *Jesus the Miracle Worker: A Historical & Theological Study* (Downers Grove, IL: IVP Academic, 1999), 108.

(4)

Restoring of a Paralytic at Capernaum

(Matthew 9:1–8; Mark 2:1–12; Luke 5:17–26)

Jesus had returned to his own town, Capernaum. He was in a home there and many people had gathered in that house. The crowd was so large that there was no more room. Among the crowd was a collection of religious leaders: the Pharisees, scribes, and teachers of the law. They had come from Galilee, Judea, and Jerusalem. Jesus was teaching the crowd in the house. His lesson was interrupted by four men who had opened a hole in the roof and dropped a paralyzed man on a mat in front of Jesus. When Jesus saw the man, he told him his sins were forgiven. This proclamation caused internal consternation for the gathered religious leaders. Jesus knew their hearts and minds. He asked them if it was easier to declare the forgiveness of sins or to perform a healing. He then responded to his own question by stating the forthcoming healing was a sign of his identity. Then Jesus told the paralyzed man to stand up, pick up his mat, and go home. When the man did just what Jesus had commanded, the gathered crowd was astonished at what they had witnessed.

The three Gospel accounts of this healing are relatively similar, with only a few differences in their descriptions. Matthew's record of this healing is the briefest. He does not mention how the paralytic got to Jesus other than to state that some men brought him there. Thus, he leaves out the dramatic scene of the four men removing parts of the house's roof and lowering the paralyzed man in front of Jesus (Mark 2:4; Luke 5:18–19). In Matthew's conclusion of the story, the crowded house responded to the forgiveness of sin by giving glory to God. This can be seen in their recognition of the authority given to Jesus (Matt 9:8). It was as if the crowd was more awestruck by the forgiveness of sin rather than the healing of the paralyzed man. Mark and Luke concluded their account of this story by emphasizing the crowd's statement of seeing strange things (Mark 2:12; Luke 5:26). It appeared that those in the house saw the entire circumstance, the healing and the forgiveness, as an unexpected and incredible happening.

The most striking similarities recorded in the three accounts of this healing are connected to what Jesus says in this event. All three writers record Jesus as saying something similar to both the gathered religious leaders and to the paralyzed man. Thus, emphasis should be placed on understanding the importance of Jesus's speech both for the forgiveness of sin and the healing of a disability. Additionally, the language Jesus used to address the lame man demonstrates his compassion toward those who are disabled.

Disability and Compassion

The paralyzed man's physical condition is best summarized by Richard C. Blight in his *Exegetical Summary of Luke 1–11*. He notes that the language used is indicative of a man who is paralyzed in one or more limbs, that the condition is permanent as a result of the inability of the muscles to function, perhaps due to a brain or spinal injury, and that one side of his body was helpless.[1]

Just as the man's physical condition was despondent, his social circumstance would have been dismal as well. J. Byzek succinctly describes the condition of the disabled in ancient Israel. She writes, "In ancient Israel . . . only one occupation was open to a person who could not walk or who was blind: begging. There were no wheelchairs. If an ancient Israelite could not walk, he crawled—or stayed indoors until he died. It was a miserable existence."[2]

The paralyzed man had one thing going for him. He had friends who must have known about Jesus's power to heal (Luke 5:17). They were committed to bringing this paralyzed man to Jesus so he would heal him. Yet, as it turned out, this man had another friend as well. Luke notes that before Jesus told the man his sins were forgiven, he called him "friend" (Luke 5:20). *Anthrōpos*, the word used here, can be understood as either "friend" or "man." *Friend* is the positive equivalent of this word. If the term is used in a negative manner, it is translated "man." Thus, *anthrōpos* is best translated in this passage as "friend" rather than "man." English translations that use word *friend* in this verse include the NET, NIV, and CSB. This translation is recognized by I. Howard Marshall, who comments that the term, as Luke uses it, may be equivalent to the word *friend* rather than the term *man*. He also notes that Luke uses *anthrōpos* with a negative connotation in Luke 22:58, 60.[3]

J. Reiling and J. L. Swellengrebel also take the position that reproach is not present here as it is in other Lukan occurrences of the word *anthrōpos*.

---

[1] Richard C. Blight, *An Exegetical Summary of Luke 1–11*, 2nd ed., Exegetical Summaries (Dallas: SIL International, 2008), 198.

[2] J. Byzek, "Jesus and the Paralytic, the Blind, and the Lame: A Sermon," *Ragged Edge* 21, no. 6 (2000): 25.

[3] I. Howard Marshall, *The Gospel of Luke*, New International Greek Testament Commentary 3 (Grand Rapids: Eerdmans, 1978), 214.

Thus, it is best interpreted as *friend* rather than *man*.[4] Similarly, Blight indicates that Luke's use of *anthrōpos* is representative of "a friendly term used for someone who was not personally known."[5]

Further adding to the affection demonstrated by Jesus toward the paralyzed man is the way both Matthew and Mark record Jesus calling the man "son" (Matt 9:2; Mark 2:5). Donald Alfred Hagner notes that Matthew's record of Jesus using the word *son* in this healing event is in reference to the intimate way this term can be understood when it is directed toward an adult.[6] Brooks affirms that the use of *son* here is a term of endearment and should not be construed as implying anything about the age of the paralyzed man.[7]

Francois Bovon believes considering all three biblical records of this event reveals that Jesus addressed the paralyzed man in a fatherly manner.[8] When these details are combined, it adds up to a grand image of Jesus's view of this paralyzed man. Jesus viewed this man as a friend. He had compassion for him in much the same way a father is kindhearted toward his children. While Jesus did not know the man, he had concern for him and was not put off by the man's disability or the way he forced his disability upon Jesus. The man's insertion into the house and crowd was not met with a word of reproach but with a word of divine empathy.

Healing and Forgiveness

What Jesus provided this paralyzed man was more than just compassion and physical healing. He also imparted to him the forgiveness of sins. It

---

[4] J. Reiling and J. L. Swellengrebel, *A Translator's Handbook on the Gospel of Luke*, Helps for Translators, vol. 10 (Leiden, NL: Brill, 1971), 241.

[5] Blight, *An Exegetical Summary of Luke 1–11*, 199.

[6] Donald Alfred Hagner, *Matthew 1–13*, Word Biblical Commentary, vol. 33a (Dallas: Word, 1993), 232.

[7] Brooks, *Mark*, 58 (see chap. 3, n. 17). Similarly, *son* is used by Paul in 1 Tim 1:18 and 2 Tim 2:1 as a term of endearment for Timothy.

[8] François Bovon, *Luke*, Hermeneia (Minneapolis: Fortress, 2002), 179.

is this provision that ultimately drives this miracle story. Darrell L. Bock summarizes that the way Luke structures his account of this story by placing it alongside of the healing of the leper is indicative of two elements of Jesus's ministry: he has come to provide healing from the physical ills, and to provide spiritual restoration. Consequently, a story that involves both of these elements uses physical healing to prove the identity of the one who is providing spiritual restoration.[9]

It is this connection that helps shape an understanding of Jesus's perspective of disability, forgiveness, and inclusion. The condition of paralysis would have prevented this man from access to the temple. In an event only recorded by Matthew, Jesus welcomed the blind and the lame into the temple courts (Matt 21:14–17). This event took place right after Jesus had cleansed the temple by overturning the tables of the money changers and chasing them out of the area. While he was chasing them out, he was welcoming in those who were lame and blind. Those with these disabilities were healed by Jesus. Matthew further develops the confrontation Jesus has with the religious leaders by noting those he had chased out of the temple complex and those he was welcoming into the temple complex.

Craig L. Blomberg argues that Jesus was rejecting the laws that may have prevented people who were deemed as ritually impure from being welcomed in the temple. These laws find their basis in a reading of 2 Sam 5:8 in the Septuagint where the lame and blind, who are despised by David, are prevented from entering "into the house of the LORD" (GNT). Further, Blomberg argues that in casting out money changers and those who sold the sacrificial animals, Jesus was illustrating Hos 6:6 and God's desire for mercy over sacrifice. In his estimation, an appropriate ministry for the temple was the healing of the blind and lame rather than the price gauging related to the changing of currency and the sacrifice of animals.[10]

---

[9] Darrell L. Bock, *Luke*, Baker Exegetical Commentary on the New Testament, vol. 3 (Grand Rapids: Baker, 1994), 488–89.

[10] Craig L. Blomberg, *Matthew*, New American Commentary, vol. 22 (Nashville: Broadman, 1992), 316.

Craig S. Keener, agreeing with Blomberg, asserts that teachings from the *Mishnah Hagiga* and other Jewish traditions prevented these lame and blind individuals from entering the temple. He notes that this exclusion is most likely an extension of the purity laws that prevented priests from participating in certain Levitical duties (Lev 21:17–18). In Keener's estimation, it is quite likely that by the time of Jesus, this exclusion had expanded so that any individual who was lame or blind was prohibited from entering the temple. Thus, Matthew was heightening Jesus's confrontation with the religious leaders and the way they were going about the work of God in the temple.[11]

In the article "The Exegetical Dimensions of Restrictions on the Blind and the Lame in the Texts from Qumran," Saul L. Olyan notes that several Qumran texts address prohibitions against the lame and blind:

> In 11QT 45:12–14, the blind may not enter the holy city. According to 1QSa 2:3–9, the blind and the lame among others with bodily imperfections or impurities, may not present themselves in the congregation of the men of renown. In 1QM 7:4–5, the blind and the lame, along with others having permanent blemishes or polluting conditions, are forbidden from participating in the eschatological war.[12]

One can see these restrictions played out in Acts 3:1–26 where a man who was lame from birth was begging outside of the temple and was approached by Peter and John. This location, outside of the temple gate, was as close as a crippled person could get to the temple. Consequently, their ability to receive the forgiveness of sin was severely impacted. They could not enter the temple complex and offer any of the prescribed sacrifices for their sin.

Taking these restrictions into consideration, the paralyzed man, who was brought to Jesus on a mat, was presented first with the one thing he

---

[11] Craig S. Keener, *The Gospel of Matthew: A Socio-Rhetorical Commentary* (Grand Rapids: Eerdmans, 2009), 502.

[12] Saul M. Olyan, "The Exegetical Dimensions of Restrictions on the Blind and the Lame in Texts from Qumran," *Dead Sea Discoveries* 8, no. 1 (2001): 38.

could not experience—the forgiveness of his sins. It was his greatest need. Jesus's pronouncement of forgiveness was a demonstration that all sinners, regardless of their ability or disability, have access to the forgiveness of God.

This miracle story highlights the importance of seeing the forgiveness of sin and the healing from disability as two separate events. Amos Yong notes the basis provided by the Gospel writers for this healing was so that the religious leaders would know Jesus had the authority to forgive sins. The distinction between the act of forgiving sin and healing was in keeping with the predominant need of the other parties in the story.[13] Quoting Kerry Wynn from an unpublished paper, Yong writes, "Forgiveness was for the sake of the faithful person with a disability; the healing was a sign for the unbelieving religious leaders."[14]

Block recognizes this same point when she insists that Jesus removed the man's disability to demonstrate that he was God. There was no need to remove the paralyzed man's disability to forgive his sin. It was the forgiveness of sin that was more important than the removal of paralysis. God's forgiveness of our sin, in whatever state an individual is in, should provide comfort.[15]

While disability appears to prevent temple access to the forgiveness rituals, it was not prohibitive to Jesus's extension of God's eternal forgiveness administered through Christ. Jesus's interaction with the paralyzed man demonstrates a personal desire that forgiveness and inclusion be extended to the disabled. Further, by welcoming them into the temple, much to the chagrin of the religious leaders, Jesus was demonstrating the inclusive nature of God's kingdom. In this kingdom those who are blind and lame are admitted and healed. Their acceptance leaves those who practice exclusion to wonder about the nature of this new kingdom.

---

[13] Amos Yong, *The Bible, Disability, and the Church: A New Vision of the People of God* (Grand Rapids: Eerdmans, 2011), 60–61.

[14] Yong, 61.

[15] Block, *Copious Hosting*, 108 (see chap. 1, n. 6).

(5)

Restoring of a Man with a Withered Hand

(Matthew 12:9–14; Mark 3:1–6; Luke 6:6–11)

Jesus entered a synagogue on a Sabbath and commenced teaching. Among those in attendance was a man who had a withered right hand. A collection of scribes and Pharisees was also there that day. These religious leaders were focused on Jesus, as they were looking for a way to accuse him. More specifically, they believed Jesus would heal the man with a withered hand with no regard for the Sabbath. Jesus posed a question to them. His question was about good or evil and life or death. He asked if it was lawful to do good on the Sabbath. Further, was it acceptable to save a life or to kill? The religious leaders said nothing and offered no response. Jesus looked around at them with a mix of anger and sorrow. He knew the hardness of their hearts. Jesus turned his attention back to the man with the withered hand. He told him to stretch out his hand. When the man did as he was commanded, his hand was restored so that it was as good as the other.

Immediately the religious leaders left the synagogue, found the Herodians, and joined forces to plot against the destruction of Jesus.

The story of the restoration of a withered hand is a miracle story that is as much about Jesus's conflict with the religious leaders as it is about the healing of a disabled man. Indeed, like the story of the paralyzed man who was brought to Jesus, this healing serves as the method of confrontation. Jesus's question to the scribes and Pharisees followed by the healing of the withered hand reveals as much about Jesus's ministry and the nature of the kingdom as it relates to those who are disabled.

Of the three Gospel accounts of this story, Mark and Luke share the greatest resemblance. The majority of the differences are recorded in the center verses of Matthew's account of this healing. Matthew places a first question about the lawfulness of healing on the Sabbath as coming from the religious leaders. Jesus responded to this question by offering an example and then an answer to their question. Using the example of a sheep that had fallen into a pit to challenge their question, he gave the corresponding answer that it is lawful to do good on the Sabbath (Matt 12:11–12). Mark and Luke say nothing about the example of the sheep. Conversely, Matthew says nothing about Jesus's additional question on saving a life or destroying a life (Mark 3:4; Luke 6:9).

Taken as a whole, these three stories reveal something about divine love and mercy, which is highlighted by the way Mark reports Jesus's response to the Pharisees scheming and silence. Separately, Matthew's account offers us a glimpse into the value of a human life that is beset by disability. Together, the accounts provided by Mark and Luke reveal something of the nature of Jesus's ministry and its connection to the new kingdom.

Divine Love and Mercy

At face value this story easily establishes the mercy and love demonstrated in the actions of Jesus Christ as opposed to the ruthlessness modeled by the religious leaders. Their strict interpretation of Sabbath law prohibited them from extending mercy to one who was in need. Rather than looking at this man with an eye toward mercy, they looked at this man with a view to exploiting his plight as a means to trap Jesus. However, as noted by John Nolland, Jesus's approach to keeping the Sabbath is strikingly different than the religious leaders. His view was ruled by the premise that loving God is indivisible from loving your neighbor. Thus, if an action dishonors a neighbor, then it cannot be the kind of action that brings honor to God. Additionally, any inaction that leaves a neighbor in suffering can only be regarded as evil.[1]

William L. Lane stresses this point as well. He insists the religious leaders' concern for legal details came at the expense of compassion and kindness. As such, these Pharisees had forgotten that God's provision of the Sabbath was an example of mercy and grace. Their pious approach to Sabbath keeping had caused them to become unmoved by the purposes of God and the sufferings of men.[2] Jesus saw that loving the man with the withered hand enough to heal him was a demonstration of loving God "with all your heart, with all your soul, with all your mind, and with all your strength" (Mark 12:30 NKJV).

The attitude of the religious leaders toward Jesus's healing on the Sabbath would eventually be expressed in Luke 13:10–16. In this story, Jesus heals a woman who has been disabled by a back issue for eighteen years. Immediately after this healing, the annoyed synagogue leader responds in outrage by saying, "There are six days when work should be done; therefore come on those days and be healed and not on the Sabbath day" (Luke 13:14 CSB).

The religious leaders clearly had an understanding that even healing on the Sabbath, when life or death was not at stake, should be avoided at all costs. The regular pattern of life afforded many additional occasions for

---

[1] John Nolland, *Luke 1–9:20*, Word Biblical Commentary, vol. 35a (Dallas: Word, 1989), 263.

[2] William L. Lane, *The Gospel According to Mark*, New International Commentary on the New Testament (Grand Rapids: Eerdmans, 1974), 124.

healing in the six other days, rather than treading on Sabbath protocol to obtain healing.

The contrast between the mercy offered by Jesus and the role of the religious leaders in this story is also highlighted by their immediate response to the man with the paralyzed hand. Both Mark and Luke note that the Pharisees were "watching him closely" (Mark 3:2; Luke 6:7 CSB). Guelich recognizes the malicious intentions of these men as he identifies the word *watching* (Gk. *pareteroun*) as having connotations toward lying in wait for someone. They intend to use this man and this opportunity to catch Jesus in the act of a Sabbath violation.[3] Marvin R. Vincent develops this meaning further by arguing that the phrase "they kept watching" (CEV) implies "one who dogs another's steps, keeping beside or near him." Further, he agrees with Wycliffe's translation that "played the spy" is a suitable rendering of this phrase.[4] Bock concurs and notes the emotive quality of "watching" has a sinister attribute where it would mean "to spy on or watch out of the corner of one's eye" or "to watch lurkingly." For Bock, the imagery here is similar to something that would be used in our contemporary spy novel.[5]

Jesus's intention was to heal the paralyzed man. The immediate intention of these religious leaders was to spy ominously on Jesus and catch him in a legal trap. For Jesus, the presence of the man with the paralyzed hand was an opportunity to display the compassion and mercy of God. For the scribes and Pharisees, this same encounter was not a moment for mercy but the perfect chance to prove, once and for all, that this healer was not from God because he willfully violated the Sabbath commands of God.

Mark's account of this story also provides us with one more glimpse of the religious leaders' lack of mercy. He tells us that Jesus became emotional

---

[3] Guelich, *Mark*, 134 (see chap. 3, n. 12).

[4] Marvin R. Vincent, *Word Studies in the New Testament Volumes I: The Synoptic Gospels; Acts of the Apostles; Epistles of Peter, James & Jude*, 2nd ed., vol. 1 (Grand Rapids: Eerdmans, 1977), 175.

[5] Bock, *Luke*, 528–29 (see chap. 4, n. 9).

at the silence of the Pharisees to his question on doing good or evil and saving a life or killing on the Sabbath. Mark notes that Jesus's reaction to this
silence was anger that turned to sorrow over their hearts (Mark 3:5). Mark
employs the word *pōrōsis* to describe the hard hearts of the religious leaders
who were present in the synagogue. Not only were their mouths silent, their
hearts were hard.

Kenneth Samuel Wuest picturesquely describes *pōrōsis* as the covering
over of something with a thick layer of skin. He also indicates that *pōrōsis*
can be understood as a hardening that is covered with a callus. Biblically,
he sees the word pointing to dense mental perception or a dulled sense of
discernment. Contextually, he clarifies that the hardness of the Pharisees
hearts represents a moral and spiritual obtuseness rather than a mental
one.[6] Rodney Cooper vividly explains that *pōrōsis* is a medical term used
for describing how doctors went about mending a broken bone. Thus, the
image created by Mark is of a heart so hard that it cannot be softened. For
healing to occur it would need to be broken. Cooper argues that this hardness of heart is an attitudinal sin with a fixed outlook against God.[7] Vincent
also connects *pōrōsis* to the field of medicine by stating that it was through
callousness that bones were mended together. However, he also notes this
word was used as a descriptor for a certain kind of marble.[8]

Mark's description of the Pharisees presents a group of men who
were incapable of demonstrating mercy and compassion. Their hearts had
become so hardened that matters of moral and spiritual significance would
not stir empathy within them. Their fastidious commitment to following the letter of the law had so hardened their hearts that they could not
understand the spirit of the law. Their inaction, marked by silence and hard

---

[6] Kenneth Samuel Wuest, *Wuest's Word Studies from the Greek New Testament
for the English Reader, Vol 1: Mark, Romans, Galatians, Ephesians and Colossians*
(Grand Rapids: Eerdmans, 1973), 65.

[7] Rodney Cooper, *Mark,* Holman New Testament Commentary, vol 2
(Nashville: B&H, 2000), 50.

[8] Vincent, *Word Studies in the New Testament,* 1:175.

hearts, stands in opposition to the merciful heart of Jesus that must do good regardless of the day.

In this pericope, Jesus's heart is one that resonates divine compassion. Conversely, the hearts of the religious leaders were calculated and calloused. They stubbornly refused to recognize the mercy of God behind the healing miracles of Jesus. This refusal was even more true when these miracles butted up against their imposed Sabbath conventions. Divine love and mercy meet at the crossroads of this healing miracle. The Gospel writers set Jesus's question and subsequent healing of the man with the paralyzed hand against the inaction of the religious leaders. This juxtaposition reveals how the presence of mercy is a hallmark of Jesus's demonstration of what it looks like to love God and love others. Conversely, those who are content to establish and promote Sabbath-keeping laws find within themselves the inability to be conduits of grace and mercy for those who are hurting.

Disability and the Value of Human Life

The man in this story is described as having a withered right hand (Luke 6:6 ESV). Two things should be noted about his disabled condition based on this description. First, Leon Morris points out that the atrophied hand would be unsightly, cause personal discomfort, and hinder the man's ability to earn a living. The last of these descriptions is reinforced by the fact that it was the man's right hand that was withered.[9] Edwards graphically describes the condition of this man's hand by noting that the range of meaning for "shriveled" (Gk. *xērainō*) includes "dried up," "withered," and "stiff." Consequently, a hand that is both stiff and deformed fits the description of this man's paralyzed hand.[10] With an inability to use his right hand, this man has become left-handed. Gordon Jensen describes both the theological and social shame associated with being left-handed in biblical culture:

---

[9] Leon Morris, *The Gospel According to Matthew*, Pillar New Testament Commentary (Grand Rapids: Eerdmans, 1992), 305.

[10] Edwards, *The Gospel According to Mark*, 99 (see chap. 3, n. 13).

The traditional bias against the left hand in scripture and in ancient society is fairly obvious. The identification of the left hand with the place of evil and of rejection (e.g., Mt 25:31–46) is contrasted to the honor given the right hand. The right-hand symbolized blessing (Gen 48:12), power and might (Is 48:13), great friendship (Gal 2:9), and the special place of honor (Mk 12:36, 1 Kgs 2:19); while the left-hand signified weakness, deception, and treachery. The right hand is portrayed as the prominent and good hand of God, while the left hand is either subservient to it or its antithesis. . . . This was a strong social stigma in the mid-east, especially since the left hand was the hand used for personal hygiene. To use the left hand, therefore, was to show one's weakness and shame. It was to be cursed by society.[11]

Further, William Hendriksen, quoting the apocryphal *Gospel According to the Hebrews*, identifies this man as a former stonemason who must now resort to the life of a beggar. Hence, he was appealing to Jesus for help by restoring his hand so he could abandon the life of a beggar.[12] Considering all of this, the stigma of disability was a grand obstacle for this man. He was disgraced three times over. He had a disabled hand, he was forced to become left-handed in a culture that viewed left-handedness with disdain, and he must resort to the social position of beggar to survive.

Each of these elements are important because they establish the social value of the man with the paralyzed hand. He offered nothing to community life and could best be regarded as an object of charity. This man clearly needed help. However, the religious leaders viewed him simply as the perfect means to trap Jesus with a legal question. This question centered around what was lawful to do on a Sabbath day. On three previous occasions

---

[11] Gordon Jensen, "Left-Handed Theology and Inclusiveness—Liberty University," *Horizons* 17, no. 2 (1990): 207–8, https://doi.org/10.1017/S0360966900020168.

[12] William Hendriksen, *Exposition of the Gospel According to Matthew*, Baker New Testament Commentary (Grand Rapids: Baker, 1973), 516.

Jesus healed someone on the Sabbath. He healed a man with an unclean spirit (Mark 1:21–28), he healed Peter's mother-in-law (Matt 8:14–15; Mark 1:29–31; Luke 4:38–39), and he healed the lame man at the pool of Bethesda (John 5:1–18). Presumably, the word of Jesus's Sabbath healings had created a concern for the religious leaders who had now gathered in the synagogue. Their question, "Is it lawful to heal on the Sabbath?" (Matt 12:10 NIV) was designed to find out if he would heal again on a Sabbath day.

Jesus entered the discussion by using an example from lesser to greater. He intended to compare the value of an animal to the value of a human being. Twelftree recognizes that Jesus was not appealing to any one law in particular. Rather, Jesus was addressing the generally favorable manner in which the Jews treated their animals.[13] If an animal could be rescued on the Sabbath, should it not follow that a man could be healed on the Sabbath? Jesus's argument not only challenged what the religious leaders valued, but also the way they were enforcing Sabbath regulations. Craig S. Keener contends that the only religious group that would not have permitted the rescue of an animal on the Sabbath was the Essenes. Consequently, many of the Pharisees would have agreed with Jesus and asserted it was lawful to save an animal that had fallen into a pit. Jesus's proposition, then, is if one has concern for a sheep on the Sabbath, how much more should the same amount of concern be shown to a person?[14] To put Keener's words into a simpler statement, if the religious leaders would do good by helping a sheep who has only little value, why should Jesus not do good by healing this man?

It is easy to become so enamored with how Jesus called into question the way the religious leaders applied Sabbath law that one misses the statement Jesus made about the value of a human being with a disability. Jesus did not discount or devalue this man because of his disability. Categorization through social status would have determined this man had

---

[13] Twelftree, *Jesus the Miracle Worker*, 126 (see chap 3, n. 21).

[14] Craig S. Keener, *The IVP Bible Background Commentary: New Testament*, 2nd ed. (Downers Grove, IL: IVP Academic, 2014), 76.

little worth. Consequently, he would have been relegated to a place of insignificance. Similarly, the religious leaders would have questioned this man's usefulness. These leaders would have ascribed little, if any, value to him. Indeed, using Jesus's own example, some of these leaders might have even suggested the animal had more value, as it could at least contribute something to society. However, Jesus acknowledged that this man still had the same value every human being has. Hendriksen poignantly summarizes Jesus's point:

> If on the Sabbath doing good to an animal is allowed, then all the more it is right and proper on that day to show kindness to a man, God's image-bearer! . . . Certainly, because man is incomparably more valuable in the sight of God than a sheep. Therefore, it is right to do good on the Sabbath, that is, to be a blessing to man, not to remain indifferent to his needs.[15]

Not only had Jesus called into question the way the religious leaders were legislating Sabbath observance; he was calling into question the way they were failing to ascribe value and dignity to human beings. For Jesus, the man with the paralyzed hand was not an object lesson for a debate, nor was he simply a subject for charity. He was a human being whose value, regardless of his disability, rested in the fact that he had within him the *imago Dei*.

The Nature of Jesus's Ministry: Healing and Salvation

One final exploration into this story should be undertaken. Both Mark and Luke add that Jesus's question on doing good also included a question on saving a life or killing (Mark 3:4; Luke 6:9). It is possible to consider this additional question as a reflection of Jesus's foreknowledge of the religious leaders' future plans against him (Mark 3:6; Luke 6:11). Hendriksen succinctly summarizes this point when he states that Jesus's dual question

---

[15] Hendriksen, *Exposition of the Gospel According to Matthew*, 517.

essentially asks, "Is it right on the Sabbath to do good and to save life, as I am doing; or to do harm and to destroy, as you are right now doing."[16]

Another possibility for explaining the second half of Jesus's question ("to save life or to destroy it"; Luke 6:9 NIV) is related to the connection between this healing and the salvific restoration of Jesus's ministry. Jesus used this opportunity to expand on what it means to "save a life." Since the man with the withered hand was not in jeopardy of dying, it is difficult to understand this question as Jesus preventing this man from dying in the immediate future. At best, one may argue that this is a quality-of-life issue. If this is correct, Jesus's comment on saving a life has to do with saving this man's quality of life. To be sure, removing the stigma of disability would be a very dramatic change to one quality of life during biblical culture. However, the first portion of Jesus's question addresses the quality-of-life issue. The question of doing good on a Sabbath more than accounts for improving this man's quality of life by way of healing. The question still remains, then, how can Jesus mean that healing a man with a withered hand is akin to saving a life?

Guelich postulates that this question centers around the purpose of Jesus's ministry, which is summarized in Mark 1:15, where Jesus proclaims, "The time is fulfilled, and the kingdom of God has come near. Repent and believe the good news!" (CSB). Consequently, when Jesus asked the two questions about doing good and saving a life, he was thinking eschatologically. He was connecting the forthcoming healing to the day of salvation and the fulfillment of God's promised activity in history (Matt 11:5; Luke 7:22). This is precisely what Jesus came to carry out with both his words and his actions. Guelich concludes that "God's redemptive rule is realized in the making whole of a person."[17]

Similarly, Joel B. Green argues that Luke's use of "to save" and "to restore" are cues pointing toward the way "to save life" fits Jesus's argument.

---

[16] William Hendriksen, *Exposition of the Gospel According to Luke*, Baker New Testament Commentary (Grand Rapids: Baker, 1978), 323.

[17] Guelich, *Mark*, 136, quoting Dietzfelbinger in *Evangelische Theologie*.

Green holds that, in the Greco-Roman culture, "to save" carried with it the idea of rescue from a perilous circumstance. This notion was extended to more than just physical situations or medical illnesses. Additionally, in the restoration of the man's hand (Luke 6:10), Luke uses the word *apokathistēmi* to describe the outcome of the healing. This same word is used in the Septuagint for the restoration of Israel. While Luke is not connecting the restoration of all of Israel to the healing of this man's hand, he is pointing to the eschatological reality that Jesus has in mind here. For Jesus, this day was a day of salvation for the man with a withered hand.[18]

As Green and Guelich have argued, Jesus saw this moment as a moment of faith for the man with a paralyzed hand. His interaction with Jesus in the synagogue was a life-or-death situation. To be obedient to Christ's command would lead to more than just the restoration of his hand. This man's relationship to God, through the healing word of Jesus Christ, would be restored as well. In the truest sense, Jesus was saving this man's life.

Once again, the implications of this story speak to those within the disabled community as well as those outside of this community. Jesus's interaction with this man shows the value that is ascribed to all human beings. This value is not just a reality for those who are able-bodied. Jesus's demonstration of mercy challenges Christians to show the same kind of compassion their Lord expresses here. To do otherwise places them in the camp of the religious leaders. Finally, the call to faith extended by Jesus to the man with the withered hand reveals the necessity of matching acts of mercy with the message of salvation. It is not enough for those who follow Christ to show mercy toward those who are disabled. They must recognize that having a disability does not disqualify or prevent a person from stretching out a hand and taking hold of the gift of God's grace.

---

[18] Joel B. Green, *The Gospel of Luke*, New International Commentary on the New Testament (Grand Rapids: Eerdmans, 1997), 256.

6

Curing of a Woman with Twelve-Year Bleeding

(Matthew 9:20–22; Mark 5:25–34; Luke 8:43–48)

Jesus had just arrived on the other side of the sea. As he stepped off the boat, a large crowd began to gather around him. In this crowd was a leader of the synagogue named Jairus. He had a matter of utmost importance that he needed to discuss with Jesus. His twelve-year-old daughter was sick. Jairus desired the healing help of Jesus so that she would live. Jesus, the disciples, and the large crowd all headed to Jairus's house.

While they were on the way, a woman who had a disorder that caused her to bleed slipped into the crowd. This disorder had plagued her for the past twelve years. Though she had sought the help of many doctors, no remedy was found. In her mind, however, she believed if she could only touch Jesus, she would be made well. Approaching Jesus from behind, she touched the edge of his clothing and was immediately made well. Instantly,

Jesus knew something had happened. Someone had touched him. He felt the power of God flow out of him. He stopped and asked, "Who touched me?" The disciples did not understand Jesus's question. The crowd was so large that Jesus was inadvertently being touched by quite a few people. The woman knew she had been found out and in fear fell down in front of Jesus. She told him the truth about what she had done. Jesus responded by calling her "daughter" and commented that her faith had made her well. Then Jesus told her to leave in peace.

While all of this was taking place, people from Jairus's house arrived to tell him that they did not need to bother Jesus anymore. Jairus's daughter had died. When Jesus overheard the conversation, he told the synagogue leader not to be afraid and encouraged him to continue believing. When they arrived at Jairus's house, Jesus asked why there was such mourning going on. He told the people gathered at the house that the girl was not dead but asleep. The people laughed. Jesus asked them all to leave the house. He took the girl's parents, as well as Peter, James, and John, and went to where the girl was lying. He reached out, took the girl by the hand, and said, "Little girl, get up." The girl did just as Jesus had asked. Those gathered around were amazed. Jesus told them two things. First, they needed to get her some food. Second, they were not to tell anyone about this miracle.

The stories of these two healing miracles are recorded with some detail in both Mark and Luke. Their presentations are quite similar, so that when taken together, one gets the addition of small details that enhance and color the story. Matthew presents both stories as well, but his account is much more concise and offers no details of consequence that are not presented in the other two accounts. There is also little by way of textual analysis that needs to be brought out as distinguishing marks between the Markan and Lucan accounts of these two stories. Instead, a more profitable textual analysis occurs between the way both writers position the healing of the hemorrhaging woman in an interchange with the healing of Jairus's daughter.

According to James R. Edwards, Mark specifically uses this technique to draw attention to the middle story that is sandwiched between the beginning and ending of the first story. In doing so, Mark is taking a literary technique and using it to showcase his theological purpose. Edwards believes Mark employed this technique nine times in his Gospel to highlight themes of faith, discipleship, bearing witness, and the dangers of apostasy.[1]

Robin Branch notes that by flipping between one story and then the other, Mark intends for the reader to notice comparisons and contrasts between the two stories. Further, Branch provides one of the most thorough lists of similarities and differences between these two stories. She notes that the comparisons and contrasts include things like Jairus's lofty position as a member of the synagogue and the woman's position as a crowd member and societal outcast. Both Jairus and the woman are portrayed with a sense of urgency in their need for Jesus's assistance. Branch lists Jairus as ritually clean and the woman as ritually unclean and impure. Jairus's position probably afforded him a great deal of wealth, while the woman was potentially penniless from seeking a cure for her ailment. Further, Jairus spoke to Jesus face-to-face to request healing, while the woman silently approached Jesus from behind and took her healing. However, both this woman and Jairus's daughter experienced healing through touch.[2]

While only one story is truly a story of disability as is defined in this study, both stories will be considered. This consideration rests on the fact that these two stories draw out three important observations with regard to Jesus's ministry and inclusive leadership. First, these two stories serve to show a meaningful contrast that demonstrates maximum inclusion in Jesus's ministry. Second, these two stories highlight the way Jesus grows and matures the faith of two individuals. Finally, in the center story, that of the hemorrhaging woman, we see a connection being forged between faith and salvation through the avenue of healing.

---

[1] James R. Edwards, "Markan Sandwiches. The Significance of Interpolations in Markan Narratives," *Novum Testamentum* 31, no. 3 (1989): 196, https://doi.org/10.2307/1560460.

[2] Robin Branch, "Literary Comparisons and Contrasts in Mark 5:21–43," *In Die Skriflig/In Luce Verbi* 48 (March 20, 2014): 2, https://doi.org/10.4102/ids.v48i1.1799.

A Meaningful Contrast

The first and most obvious point of observation is how Jesus's ministry is portrayed as reaching those at both the highest and the lowest levels of the social spectrum. As a synagogue leader, Jairus was in a much different position than the hemorrhaging woman. Thus, one point being made through interchange is this difference. Branch postulates that, while it would appear Jairus and the hemorrhaging woman were about the same age and lived in the same town, they did not know each other. Additionally, his wealth and role as a synagogue leader combined with her life as a poor outcast placed them in different social circles. These circles share no real connecting point other than their physical need for healing. They both understood that this need can only be met in Jesus.[3]

Both Mark and Luke refer to Jairus as a leader in the synagogue. Bock provides a brief character sketch of Jairus. He connects Jairus's status as a ruler in the synagogue to the person responsible for arranging services as well as order and progress in worship. While this would not have made him a civil leader or a member of the Sanhedrin, it did make him a man of social standing and a leader of the city.[4] Guelich adds to this by noting that Jairus was probably responsible for overseeing building-related matters at the synagogue as well. As such, this elected position was one of esteem in the Jewish community.[5] Nolland concludes that Jairus represents the Jewish establishment and is an official representative of Judaism.[6]

This description pales in comparison to the hemorrhaging woman. She would not be afforded the same type of social status because of her illness. Bock believes that her condition would have equated to her being continuously unclean, constantly embarrassed, as well as shut out from fellowship and religious life.[7] Leon Morris spells out what life may have been like for this woman:

---

[3] Branch, 3.

[4] Bock, *Luke*, 792 (see chap. 4, n. 9).

[5] Guelich, *Mark*, 295 (see chap. 3, n. 12).

[6] Nolland, *Luke. 1–9*, 419 (see chap. 5, n. 1).

[7] Bock, *Luke*, 794.

The malady itself must have been distressing and it had social consequences as well as physical. Because this complaint made her ceremonially unclean (Lev. 15:25), the sufferer was not permitted to take any part in temple worship or the like. Her uncleanness was readily communicable to other people (a touch was all that was needed, Lev. 15:27). She would accordingly have been avoided lest others contract from her an uncleanness which, though temporary, was troublesome. Life must have been very difficult.[8]

Morris's description highlights the social and religious consequences of her hemorrhaging by pointing out her uncleanness. One mistake that must not be made is to equate uncleanness with a loss of social status. While uncleanness had social ramifications, it did not, by itself, impact social status. Paula Fredriksen argues that first-century Jews understood three things about impurity: "First, impurity is not sin. . . . Second, in Jewish tradition, purity does not correspond to social class. . . . Third, impurity is gender blind."[9]

Her second assumption has relevance to this study. With regard to social class and impurity, she writes:

Impurity is a fact of life but not of class. The lowliest peasant who has just completed the ritual of the red heifer is pure, whereas the most aristocratic priest, having just buried a parent, is not. The fussiest Pharisee, the highest high priest, is neither more nor less *tameh* after marital intercourse than is the scruffiest Galilean fisherman. Only the priest must refrain from certain normal activities because his workplace is the Temple. To see impurity as a quasi-permanent state, and then to conflate such a state with social class, is simply wrong.[10]

---

[8] Leon Morris, *Luke: An Introduction and Commentary*, rev. ed, Tyndale New Testament Commentaries, vol. 3 (Grand Rapids: Eerdmans, 1988), 178.

[9] Paula Fredriksen, "Did Jesus Oppose the Purity Laws?" *Bible Review* 11, no. 3 (1995): 23.

[10] Fredriksen, 23.

Working from Fredriksen's assertion, the bleeding woman is not relegated to a lower social class just because of her hemorrhage. Impurity did not remove and then assign a new and lower social status. One simply needed to fulfill the necessary ritual so that being pure or clean was reestablished. While there were most definitely social ramifications because of this woman's continual bleeding, one of them was not a reassigned lower social standing.

Mark tells us she had spent everything she had on doctors, hoping to be cured. However, their help was ineffective, provided no relief, and only made her situation worse. Whatever financial means might have given her status and stability in society had also been removed. Further, no mention of family is given in any of the three Gospel accounts. Nothing is said of a husband or any other relatives. She faced her illness and her tragic life alone. There appears to be no family to offer support, financial or other, for her chronic condition. Yet even her isolation is answered in this story. After Jesus healed her, then confronted her, she heard a family description that she had probably not heard for some length of time. Jesus called her "daughter." The hemorrhaging woman was given a mark of family identification for, presumably, the first time in twelve years.

The aloneness of this woman was not inconsequential. If she was as alone as the text may indicate, she faced a placement in life that was stacked against her because of her sex. Dorothy Patterson outlines what it was like to live as a woman during this time. She points out that a woman was expected to manage the household and perform the duties of wives and mothers. They had little autonomy and were subordinate to their husbands. Thus, the woman became part of the husband's family or clan. A woman had a weaker legal position than a man in Israel. This position meant a husband could divorce his wife for "some uncleanness in her" (Deut 24:1–4 NKJV). However, no such law existed for the woman if she wanted a divorce from her husband. Additionally, a wife could be forced to perform a jealousy ritual if the husband questioned her fidelity to him. No such test was available for the wife if she doubted her husband's faithfulness. A daughter was permitted to receive the family inheritance only if there were no immediate male heirs in the family (Num 27:8–11). Otherwise, her inheritance was the dowry she received when she became married.[11]

Of note in Patterson's description are a couple of features relevant to the story of the hemorrhaging woman. It would have been legally permissible for this woman to have been married and then to be issued a certificate of divorce for her chronic uncleanness. If this were the case, it would provide an explanation for her being alone. Additionally, being a divorced woman would also add to her social stigma. Mark's account includes that she had spent all her money on doctors. Given Patterson's description, her sources of income were tied to men in a male-dominant society. It is hard to imagine this woman having a deep supply of finances dedicated to her pursuit of personal healing through medicine. Whatever she did have was likely spent quickly. Indeed, according to Mark, it had cost her all her money.

One other cultural implication should be considered given the description of the bleeding woman provided to us by Mark. How would her health impact the way society viewed her as a human being and as a woman? According to Louise Gosbell's research, the hemorrhaging woman would certainly have faced a certain level of societal rejection if her hemorrhaging was indeed tied to a menstrual disorder. Citing separate works by M. L. Edwards, Johannes Stahl, and W. K. Lacey, she puts forth the argument that during this particular time, a woman's role was defined by marriage, childbearing, and the ability to tend to her household. A woman who was not able to function in these roles was often categorized as disabled.[12] With Gosbell's research in mind, this hemorrhaging woman would fit the picture of disability, and this helps us understand her isolation. She is a

---

[11] Dorothy Patterson, "Woman," in *The Holman Illustrated Bible Dictionary*, ed. Chad Brand, Charles W. Draper, and Archie England (Nashville: Holman Bible, 2003), 1679.

[12] Louise Gosbell, "'The Poor, the Crippled, the Blind, and the Lame': Physical and Sensory Disability in the Gospels of the New Testament" (PhD diss., Macquarie University, 2015), 56–58, http://hdl.handle.net/1959.14/1107765.

disabled woman who is unable to conceive and bear children. As a consequence of this condition, she would have remained either unmarried or divorced because of this disability.

Why make such a big deal about each of these conditions? Simply put, because Mark does. To contrast the two characters in these two stories, Mark reveals just how opposite they really are. Jairus is the president of the synagogue, an elected official in a prestigious position. He is a man who has family standing, religious stature, and civic significance in his town. The hemorrhaging woman is completely and totally his opposite. She is not simply his reverse, because she is a disabled woman. The sum total of her life places her in a position of social stigma and marginalization. Where Jairus would have been embraced and celebrated, this woman was pushed aside and cast off.

Edwards acknowledges how Mark has presented the woman's ailment in such stark terms:

> In a dramatic volley of Greek participles, v. 26 graphs the woman's condition precipitously: *having* a blood flow, *having suffered* from many doctors, *having exhausted* all her wealth, *having not improved* by *having gotten worse.* The same verse is equally emphatic and categorical: she suffered *much* from *many* physicians, exhausted *all* her resources and gained *nothing.*[13]

There is a tendency to think of this woman in such a limited view that her physical condition dominates an interpretation of this passage. However, this limitation misses the depths of the comparison. Mark has provided the example of someone at the height of society and someone at the depth of society. These stories share similarities and differences despite the societal realties. However, the one true similarity in both stories is an overwhelming need for Jesus's assistance in a difficult and desperate situation.

---

[13] Edwards, *Gospel According to Mark*, 163 (see chap. 3, n. 13).

The story of the hemorrhaging woman offers hope to those whose profound disability places them on the outside of many society structures and makes them feel more left out than included. Jesus's action demonstrates that there is no difference to the access, hope, or salvation he offers. His compassion, mercy, and healing are available to any and all. The inclusive nature of Jesus's life and ministry is truly good news for those whose disability leaves them feeling like an outcast. His touch is readily available and this touch is followed by his proclamation of "son" or "daughter"—"my child!"

The Growth of Faith

A second contrast that is revealed through the interchange of these two stories is the growth of faith in Jairus and the woman with the issue of blood. Important to this discussion is how Jesus helps nurture and ripen faith. Nuria Calduch-Benages observes this growth in faith as she highlights how Jesus's power exalts the influence of faith. Both Jairus and the hemorrhaging woman have a simple but strong faith that, because of hardship, has become seasoned. Citing Franco Lambiasi, she marks the forward direction of their faith. Theirs is a faith that moved from belief in Jesus's power to heal to a faith that identified Jesus as the Messiah and the one who brings salvation.[14]

The bleeding woman's faith first appears to be almost magical in orientation. She believed that a simple touch of Jesus's clothing would heal her infirmity (Mark 5:28). Morna Dorothy Hooker attributes the woman's perception to the reports she has heard about Jesus. She also considers the logic in the woman's idea as consistent with the perception that clothing was an extension of the person. Therefore, clothing contained the same power as was manifested in the person. Further, she connects the healing of those who touched Jesus's clothing in Matt 14:34–36 and Mark 6:56 to

---

[14] N. Calduch-Benages, *Perfume of the Gospel: Jesus' Encounters with Women* (Rome: Gregorian & Biblical Press, 2012), 18.

the reports that had circulated about Jesus's power to heal.[15] In Hooker's estimation, this would be the kind of information that would have been the catalyst for a woman to venture into public and pursue healing. Allan Menzies further develops this thought by arguing that the woman viewed Jesus's touch as more than just powerful. It was sovereign. Likewise, that sovereignty extended to his clothing as well.[16]

Working through various passages of Scripture,[17] David Roach connects the corners or tassels of a person's clothing to their identity. He wonders if this scriptural knowledge, rather than magic, drove the woman to consider touching a tassel on Jesus's clothing. Chief among his speculation is the idea that this woman would have been familiar with the messianic prophecy of Mal 4:2.[18] Given that the bleeding woman's perpetual uncleanness would limit her access to important educational and ritual religious life, one would have to wonder how much she would be able to make these kinds of deep textual messianic connections.

Jesus made a point to stop the procession to Jairus's house once he realized he had been touched and power had gone out from him (Mark 5:30). He confronted the crowd in general while looking for the woman specifically. He asked, "Who touched me?" When the woman realized she had been found out, she confessed to what she had done. Jesus's response was one of compassion, calling her "daughter." Hooker believes this compassionate confrontation was designed to move the woman from a "magical" faith about Jesus into a personal relationship with Jesus.[19] Edwards argues that while the woman may have approached Jesus for either magical or

---

[15] Morna Dorothy Hooker, *The Gospel According to Saint Mark* (Peabody, MA: Hendrickson, 2009), 148.

[16] Allan Menzies, *The Earliest Gospel: A Historical Study of the Gospel According to Mark, With a Text and English Version* (New York: Macmillan, 1901), 128.

[17] See Num 15:37–41; Ruth 3:9; Ezek 16:8; 1 Sam 24:5; and Mal 4:2.

[18] David Roach, "Why Were People Healed from Touching Jesus' Clothes?," June 21, 2013, https://biblemesh.com/blog/why-were-people-healed-from-touching -jesus-clothes/.

[19] Hooker, *Gospel According to Saint Mark*, 149.

messianic means, Jesus was not content to leave this anonymous woman with just a miracle. He wanted a meeting with her. Thus, he kept looking until she came forward. Jesus's faith pronouncement connected her faith to her healing and saving.[20]

Edwards notes two very relevant observations about the actions of this woman. First, as Mark presents it in his Gospel, this woman models what it truly means to follow Jesus. She acted on what she had heard about Jesus. This example represents a discipleship pattern of she "heard," she "came," and she "touched." For Edwards this woman provided an illustration of faith that Jesus recognized and helped to further ripen as he confronted her once the healing had taken place.[21] Her faith in, and perspective of, Jesus was altered not because of the tactile healing that took place. Rather, they were transformed because of the conversation with Jesus that took place after the healing.

Edwards also explains that this woman's faith served as the immediate model for Jairus once he heard that his daughter had died. Jairus was challenged to exhibit the same faith that this woman showed. Edwards stresses that Mark's use of the word *overheard* (*parakouein*) in Mark 5:36 implies that Jesus overheard something he was not supposed to, refused to pay attention to the news, and then discounted the truth of that information. Instead, his response to Jairus implied for him to keep believing.[22]

The healing of the woman, combined with the new information presented to Jairus, serve as an example and a challenge. Jairus showed faith by coming to Jesus and requesting healing for his daughter. He also saw faith in the healing of the hemorrhaging woman. Jesus was asking him to keep believing in his power to heal despite the situation. In other words, it was as if Jesus was telling Jairus, "You have seen what I can do in a hopeless situation. I have healed someone who was as good as dead. Keep believing that I can do the same in your hopeless situation. Keep believing that I can heal

---

[20] Edwards, *Gospel According to Mark*, 164–66.

[21] Edwards, 164.

[22] Edwards, 167.

your daughter who is dead." To put it into Johannine terms, "Keep believing that I am the resurrection and the life." If Jairus had any doubts, he simply needed to look around at the recently healed woman and see the faith she had modeled in front of him.

With regard to the function of faith in the stories of Jairus and the hemorrhaging woman, two observations can be made. First, Jesus set out to purposefully mature the faith of both individuals. Second, Jesus used the display of faith from the once-disabled woman to model faith for Jairus. These two observations can have a profound impact on the church's ability to minister to those who are disabled. A pastor who seeks to lead as Jesus led will see in the hemorrhaging woman the opportunity to nurture the faith of a disabled individual. He will look for occasions where the Holy Spirit can ripen and mature that faith so that it remains strong through the circumstances of life. However, a pastor will also present those who have a disability with the chance to model faith to the church. Sadly, this is the one area that can easily be forgotten in church ministry. The challenge for the church leader is to understand how God has gifted the disabled individual and then provide the opportunity to use those gifts within the full body life of the church. In so doing, he or she will have given that individual the possibility of modeling faith to the church.

Healing, Wholeness, and Salvation

A third and final contrast drawn from these two stories centers on the issue of wholeness. In the last recorded conversation between Jesus and the woman with an issue of blood, he said to her, "Your faith has made you well. Go in peace and be free from your affliction" (Mark 5:34). This statement from Jesus addresses both the woman's physical health and her spiritual health, thus drawing together a healing that is both physical and spiritual. The peace she possessed had as much to do with the end of her physical ailment as it did with the beginning of her restored relationship to God.

Mark L. Strauss explores the semantic range of the word *well* or "to save" used in Mark 5:34. He indicates that this word can refer to spiritual salvation, physical rescue, preservation of life, or physical healing and restoration. He points out that there is a sense that physical and spiritual restoration can be perceived as synonymous in some uses of the word. Further, he argues that, theologically speaking, in the Gospels, spiritual and physical restoration go hand in hand. Thus, when Jesus made this pronouncement, these two applications can be viewed as blending together. However, he does caution against making this assumption each time the word is encountered in a biblical text.[23]

Bock underscores that the idea of peace (*eirēnē*), as Luke presents it, is not an internal or subjective feeling. Instead, peace is the state this woman found herself in because of her restored relationship to God.[24] Garland supports this perspective on peace when he connects both the physical and the spiritual through Jesus's pronouncement over the woman. He considers the biblical concept of shalom to encompass well-being, prosperity, security, friendship, and salvation. Accordingly, when Jesus pronounced peace over the woman, he was speaking to her newfound wholeness.[25] Perhaps the most concise statement on the wholeness experienced by this woman comes from Eduard Schweizer:

> And so, we arrive at Jesus's ultimate response by which he dismisses the person in peace. "Go in peace" is an Old Testament expression (Judges 17:6; 1 Samuel 1:17; 2 Samuel 15:9; but in Luke 7:50; 10:5; John 14:27; 16:33; 20:19, 21, 26) the word "peace" is synonymous with "salvation." It does not indicate peace of mind, but the objective

---

[23] Mark L. Strauss, *Mark*, Zondervan Exegetical Commentary on the New Testament (Grand Rapids: Zondervan, 2014), 232.

[24] Bock, *Luke*, 799.

[25] Garland, *Mark*, 222 (see chap. 3, n. 11).

standing of a man who, although he may be in the midst of storm and strife has been restored to a proper relationship with God.[26]

The once-disabled woman leaves the presence of Jesus being made well physically and restored to God spiritually. She was made whole. It is easy to become so focused on explaining or articulating the theological faith-healing connection that one misses the theological faith-salvation connection. This woman had a simple faith that compelled her to act on what she had heard about Jesus. It was in this response that she came to know spiritual restoration as well.

This emphasis on salvation, or the woman's restored relationship to God, offers hope for those who parent, befriend, and minister to those who are disabled. In a modern Christian culture that seems to have systematized salvation, the simple salvation that is granted here should give us pause. Today, salvation is often seen as a process that includes a more than basic theological knowledge of self, sin, Christ, and the atonement. This is followed by other outward acts, that when combined, are indicators that a person has "gotten saved" or has "given their heart to Jesus." It is to this assembly-line salvific process that this woman's story poses a challenge. She approached Jesus with little theological understanding and without any academic doctrinal knowledge. Indeed, in her perpetually unclean condition, she had little exposure to religious instruction. What she did know is that she needed help, and that Jesus was the one to offer it. It was her simple faith that Jesus pronounced had made her whole—spiritually and physically.

In a survey of salvation events in Luke-Acts (a survey that includes this story), Mark Powell surmises that salvation is "determined in each instance by the needs of the person or persons involved."[27] In other words, Luke did not see salvation as a one-size-fits-all event. Rather, salvation is first and foremost a work of God in the heart. It is he who is at work with the

---

[26] Eduard Schweizer, *The Good News According to Mark* (Atlanta: John Knox, 1970), 118.

[27] Mark Powell, "Salvation in Luke-Acts," *Word & World* 12, no. 1 (1992): 5.

knowledge and intellect available. It is his gift of grace that stirs the heart. Commenting on salvation and faith in Eph 2:8–9, John Swinton explains:

> Faith itself is not a human achievement but a grace-full gift. Therefore, unless we take a hyper-cognitive perspective on what it means to be "sure of what we hope for and certain of what we do not see," we find ourselves open to interesting new possibilities.[28]

There was nothing hyper-cognitive about the hemorrhaging woman's faith. With the grace-full gift of faith that has been given, she responded to what she knew about Jesus. In this account, then, there is hope for any parent, pastor, or caregiver who has ever wondered, "Does he know enough?" God works on the heart and dispenses the gift of grace so that even the most simple and untheological faith can bring a person face-to-face with the Savior.

---

[28] John Swinton, "Known by God," in *The Paradox of Disability: Responses to Jean Vanier and L'Arche Communities from Theology and the Sciences*, ed. Hans S. Reinders (Grand Rapids: Eerdmans, 2010), 144.

(7)

Restoring Sight to Blind Bartimaeus

(Matthew 20:29–34; Mark 10:46–52; Luke 18:35–43)

J esus was on his way to Jerusalem. He knew that the time of his death was quickly approaching. Jesus, his disciples, and the crowd that was following them were near Jerusalem when they heard a blind beggar calling out for mercy. The crowd, not wanting to be distracted, told the man to be quiet. The blind beggar did not listen. He kept on crying out, "Have mercy on me, Son of David!" Jesus stopped. It was almost as if the only word that Jesus heard above the noise of the crowd was *mercy*. Jesus asked that some people from the crowd bring the beggar to him. When those people got to the spot where the beggar was seated, they told him of his good fortune. Jesus wanted to see him. He jumped up, left his coat behind, and was brought to Jesus. Once Jesus laid his eyes on this man, he asked him, "What do you want me to do for you?" The man responded by saying, "Rabbi, Lord, I want to see." Jesus was moved with compassion. He touched the man's eyes and proclaimed that the man's faith had healed him. Immediately, Bartimaeus could see, and he gave glory to God. With his eyes healed and his sight restored, he left behind his coat and followed Jesus. Just like the beggar, the crowd responded with praise to God because of this healing.

A quick survey of the Synoptic Gospels reveals several aspects about the recording of this healing miracle. The most detailed account of the healing of blind Bartimaeus is recorded in Mark's Gospel. However, Luke's account also provides other details that add to the story. Similar to other healing narratives, Matthew's account is much more concise. In this particular story, his account adds only a couple of interesting details that are absent from the Markan and Lukan descriptions of this healing. Of primary importance in Matthew's record of this healing is his understanding of the compassion of Jesus and the tactile method of healing the blind beggar. Only Matthew tells us that Jesus was moved with compassion and that he reached out and touched the eyes of the beggar. However, all three accounts record similar statements about who Jesus is—the "Son of David." They also harmonize on both Jesus's question to the blind man and the request for sight. Each of the synoptic writers also draw attention to the crowd's insistence that the blind man be quiet, as well as his plea for mercy.

Mark's account is the more detailed of the three. It specifies the blind man's name: Bartimaeus. It also describes the response of those whom Jesus asked to bring Bartimaeus to him, Bartimaeus's response to being summoned by Jesus, and his use of the word *Rabbouni* to address Jesus. These details give it a more personal and intimate feel. One key difference between Mark and Luke's account of this healing is revealed at the end of the encounter. Mark concludes by mentioning that Bartimaeus begins to follow Jesus once he is healed. Luke points this out as well. However, Luke goes further by highlighting the fact that both the crowds and the once-blind beggar praise God for this healing.

Three observations prove valuable for disability ministry from this healing story. First, through contrasts, Bartimaeus presents us with a model of faith that is instructive for inclusion. Second, the healing of Bartimaeus demonstrates what the movement from exclusion to community looks like, and what catalyzes this movement. Finally, the multisensory component to this story challenges the minimal modality found in many worship experiences.

A Pair of Contrasts: Of Questions and Encounters

A first observation from this story centers on a pair of contrasts. The first contrast is related to a question Jesus asked, and the second contrast is related to two personal encounters with Jesus. Within literary proximity, Jesus asked on two occasions, "What do you want me to do for you?" The first time this question was posed, it was directed to two of his disciples, James and John (Mark 10:36). The second time it was asked, it was meant for blind Bartimaeus. The two responses to this question could not have been more different. The disciples of Jesus respond with a request for power and authority in Jesus's kingdom. Their answer demonstrates a continuing inability to understand just who their Rabbi is and what is his mission. On the other hand, Bartimaeus's request for healing exhibits a faith that backs up his answer to "Jesus, Son of David." Strauss believes that Jesus asked this question for two different reasons. He asked it of James and John to reveal their pride and manipulation. However, Jesus asked the same question of Bartimaeus to perceive what was behind his cry for mercy and to encourage the growth of faith.[1] To the discerning reader, the two different answers given to this question reveal that physical sight is not a guarantee of spiritual insight. James and John are more blind than Bartimaeus.

A second contrast also exists in close literary proximity. This contrast highlights the difference between the response of blind and begging Bartimaeus and a rich and young man (Mark 10:17–31). In this familiar account, a young man with much wealth approached Jesus and asked what

---

[1] Strauss, *Mark*, 472 (see chap. 6, n. 23).

he needed to do to secure salvation. After the young man detailed his law-abiding credentials, Jesus responded by telling him to sell everything he had, give the money from the proceeds to the poor, and then come follow him. Upon hearing this, the man left despondent because he had a great deal of material goods.

This narrative makes for a striking comparison to Bartimaeus, who did just what Jesus had told the young man to do. Upon being summoned to Jesus, Bartimaeus left his coat and immediately allowed some members of the crowd and/or the disciples to bring him to Jesus. At face value, it may appear that he had not given up much in this process. However, when one considers all he was leaving, he was making a similar "all" sacrifice that Jesus stressed to the young man. Kenneth E. Bailey comments on the wide range of implications for Bartimaeus if he chose healing and followed Jesus. He argues that in traditional Middle Eastern society, beggars provided a valuable service to the community. They allowed other individuals to demonstrate both charity and mercy. This demonstration showed that the giving individual was bringing alms to God by way of the beggar. In return for these alms, it was believed that God's blessing would flow out to the one giving the money. Consequently, beggars provided a valuable community service. Bailey also estimates that, as a blind beggar, Bartimaeus would have had no record of education, training, or employment. His marketable skills for the community would have been minimal. Thus, the choice to see would be a costly one. It placed him in a completely different world with new challenges and responsibilities.[2]

Bailey's implication is that the easiest thing for Bartimaeus to do was to request money from Jesus. The alms provided by Jesus would have contributed to meeting the blind beggar's daily needs. To ask for more than this, specifically healing, is a request to leave everything behind. Symbolically, this relinquishing is pictured by Bartimaeus leaving his coat to meet Jesus and then following Jesus along the way once he was healed.

---

[2] Kenneth E. Bailey, *Jesus through Middle Eastern Eyes: Cultural Studies in the Gospels* (Downers Grove, IL: IVP Academic, 2008), 173–74.

Francis J. Moloney asserts, "Narrative units are not separated by brick walls. One flows into the other, looks back to issues already mentioned, and hints at themes yet to come."[3] Thus, it is hard not to see these two contrasting examples flowing into each other. Jesus presented the same idea in these two stories. Daniel Paavola makes a similar observation. He sees in Bartimaeus's tossing aside and then leaving his cloak a direct contrast to the rich man. This man, when given the opportunity to follow Jesus, chose instead to cling to his wealth.[4] This contrast expresses the idea that those who follow Jesus are ones who are willing to leave everything behind and accept the new challenges and responsibilities that come with discipleship. This sacrifice was too much for the wealthy young man to consider. He slips off the pages of Scripture, never to be heard from again. Yet when faced with the same challenge, Bartimaeus responded to Jesus in a positive manner. Indeed, he even chose to follow Jesus rather than going his own way, as Jesus said to him.

Jesus was emphasizing the faith of Bartimaeus. He was upholding and affirming the spiritual knowledge and faith of a blind man up against that of his disciples and a successful young man. Bartimaeus's kind of faith brings one face-to-face with Jesus, the Son of David, the Messiah.

These contrasting examples ought to cause a pastor to ask, "When have I ever used a disabled person as an example of faith in my sermons?" Such a probing question will reveal a blind spot in a pastor's hermeneutical process from observation through application. If proper consideration is given to this question, it will result in a more robust exegesis of Scripture. Consequently, a pastor's congregation will be exposed to the inclusive nature of Jesus's healing and teaching ministry.

Speaking from the perspective of a pastor who is blind, Craig A. Satterlee challenges pastors to move beyond preaching the biblical accounts of people who cannot see as nothing more than sick people who need healing, sinners who need forgiveness, or an object lesson that points the way to something

---

[3] Francis J. Moloney, *The Gospel of Mark* (Peabody, MA: Hendrickson, 2002), 19.
[4] Daniel Paavola, *Mark* (St. Louis: Concordia, 2013), 196.

else. Instead, he encourages changing this oversimplified perception and helping congregations see the example of faith found in blind biblical characters like Bartimaeus. Satterlee implies that Bartimaeus's is a model of faith before he receives sight.[5]

It would be an interesting investigation to put Satterlee's last point to the test and explore how Bartimaeus's story is unpacked in most sermons. Is he chiefly an example of discipleship after he has been healed? Is he a model of faith for his ability to see what others miss about Jesus? Bartimaeus saw in Jesus, the Son of David, the one to whom he must appeal for mercy. In his blindness, he saw what every Christian, regardless of their vision, ought to recognize in the morning when they open their eyes: "Today I need to call on Jesus for mercy."

Movement: From Exclusion to Community

A second observation from this story involves the crowd mentioned in all three Gospel accounts. When we are first introduced to the crowd, they were impeding the blind beggar. In the middle of the story, they were responsible for bringing him to Jesus. In the end of the story, they can be seen glorifying God and tangentially accepting Bartimaeus as they traveled with Jesus and the disciples. This movement from exclusion to community is through the leading of Jesus.

The first impression of the crowd is not a great one. When they passed by Bartimaeus and he started pleading with Jesus for mercy, the crowd told the beggar to keep quiet. In considering their rebuke, Paavola surmises that it mirrors the disciples' rebuke of those who had brought their children to Jesus (Mark 10:13). Additionally, he envisions a scenario where Jesus was teaching as they are walking along the way and the crowd cannot hear Jesus. Thus, they told Bartimaeus to be quiet. They had come to hear Jesus, not

---

[5] Craig A. Satterlee, "Learning to Picture God from Those Who Cannot See," *Homiletic (Online)* 36, no. 1 (2011): 51–52.

him.[6] Daniel L. Akin considers their rebuke to be something close to saying, "Shut up, you fool! You are embarrassing us."[7] Block, citing the translation and commentary of Mark's Gospel by C. S. Mann, concurs and believes the crowd's disrespectful, demeaning, and rude response can be attributed to their desire to hear from Jesus as they were traveling.[8]

However, the blind beggar would not be deterred. When Jesus heard his cry for mercy, the whole procession came to a stop and Jesus requested that some of those in the crowd get Bartimaeus and bring him forward. Block argues that in this instant Jesus was moving the crowd from exclusion to inclusion. By asking the crowd to assist him, Jesus was giving them the opportunity to demonstrate the same kind of generosity and mercy he wants to show.[9] Camille Focant considers that there is, in some sense, the idea that the crowd is the subject of the first healing in this story. They are healed of their merciless bent toward exclusion before they can participate in the healing of Bartimaeus.[10] Underlying these two exchanges is the idea that these conversations are predicated on mercy. Mercy is what Bartimaeus had requested. Mercy is what the crowd was not willing to show him. Mercy was what Jesus wanted to extend to Bartimaeus, but the crowd stood in the way of this. Mercy is what Jesus showed the crowd by allowing them to participate in his extension of mercy to Bartimaeus. As a result of Jesus's actions, mercy was what the crowd ultimately showed Bartimaeus. This mercy, the mercy they had withheld only moments ago, had come to Bartimaeus from Jesus and through the crowd.

It seems fair to say that one way to move a congregation from exclusion to inclusion is through mercy. A congregation that is continuously exposed

---

[6] Paavola, *Mark*, 195.

[7] Daniel L. Akin, *Exalting Jesus in Mark*, edited by Daniel L. Akin, David Platt, and Tony Merida (Nashville: B&H, 2014), 238.

[8] Block, *Copious Hosting*, 134 (see chap. 1, n. 6).

[9] Block, 135.

[10] Camille Focant, *The Gospel According to Mark* (Eugene, OR: Pickwick, 2012), 437.

to the mercy they have received from God will seek out ways to demonstrate that mercy to others.

The blind beggar was brought to Jesus and his eyesight was restored. Jesus proclaimed that he was free to go his own way now that he had been healed. Using the same language that Jesus expressed in the healing of the hemorrhaging woman, Bartimaeus was pronounced whole. That is, he was both healed and saved. Paavola comments that Jesus rescued Bartimaeus from sinfulness as well blindness. Following Calvin's *Harmony of the Evangelists: Matthew, Mark, and Luke*, Paavola believes *faith*, as it is used here, has a double meaning. It is used to reference both the recovering of sight and the acknowledgment that Jesus is the promised Messiah from God.[11] Akin also acknowledges this dual meaning of *healed* or *saved* as it is used in Mark 10:52. He believes that Bartimaeus was healed both physically and spiritually. The proof of the physical healing was the granting of immediate sight as recorded in the text. The proof of his spiritual healing is evidenced by his desire to follow Jesus.[12]

The implication of Bartimaeus's decision to follow Jesus rather than go his own way points to his joining the crowd as they traveled to Jerusalem. In other words, he went from becoming one who was marginalized by the crowd to one who was included in the crowd. The encounter with Jesus changed both the crowd and Bartimaeus and moved them toward community. Green notes how the role of community changes because of Bartimaeus's salvation:

> Insofar as his marginal status in his community has been grounded in his physical malady, the "saving" of this man must also mark at least the potential of the reversal of his station in the community. He is not returned by Jesus to his community, however, but instead follows Jesus in discipleship; in this way, this man, formerly existing outside ordinary circles of friend and family, is identified within the

---

[11] Paavola, *Mark*, 196–97.
[12] Akin, *Exalting Jesus in Mark*, 240.

community of God's people and particularly with the "kin group" made up of Jesus and his band of followers.[13]

The implication from Green's assertion is that the community was to play a part in the discipleship of Bartimaeus. He would continue traveling with the crowd and learn from Jesus and the community along the journey to Jerusalem. The immediate lesson the community learned was one about mercy and faith. Both the crowd and Bartimaeus responded in praise to God. Thus, the crowd went from rebuking to inviting and from inviting to praising because of the mercy Jesus displayed. The geographical direction of the crowd may have been toward Jerusalem, but the spiritual direction of the crowd was away from exclusion and toward inclusion.

Multisensory Communication

A third observation from this story is not necessarily tied to the actions of Jesus, but to the way the Scriptures unfold the whole encounter. It is easy to see this story though the single lens of blindness and sight due to Bartimaeus's physical condition. However, the whole story unfolds in a multisensory perspective that should not be missed. Yong, working from Luke's account of this story, writes:

> Let's re-read the Lukan narrative of the blind man (Luke 18:35–43) as a case in point of the multisensory modalities and the multi-dimensional activities in and through which he witnessed (to) the presence and activity of God. (1) While *sitting* on the roadside, he is nevertheless not entirely passive: he is *begging*. (2) He *hears* the crowd going by, and *asks* what's going on. (3) His persistence results in his *being brought* or *led* to Jesus (by others). (4) He *persists in shouting*, "Jesus, Son of David, have mercy on me!" and when asked by Jesus what he wants, *replies*, "Lord, let me see again." (5) Upon receiving his sight, he *follows* Jesus and *glorifies* God. Note that the

---

[13] Green, *Gospel of Luke*, 665 (see chap. 5, n. 18).

blind man bears witness to the wondrous works of God not only in receiving his sight at the command of the Spirit-anointed Son of God, but also in exhibiting faith—as manifest in his alertness, aggressiveness, and response. Note also that his healing is mediated by those around him who took the time to witness to and interact with him (leading him to Jesus), and then rejoice with him.[14]

If consideration is given to the other Gospel accounts, one could add to Yong's summary that Jesus felt compassion and touched the blind beggar. At surface level, this is an encounter with Jesus that leads to a worship experience. However, it is fair to ask, do our worship services exhibit the same kind of multisensory modalities that are disability friendly? Rick Blackwood argues that God is a multisensory communicator. He notes that this can be seen in the multisensory nature of both natural and special revelation. Further, he believes that in using things like vines, branches, coins, water, wheat, and wheat fields, Jesus is using visual imagery to picturesquely communicate divine truth to his listeners. Still further, Blackwood sees within the two ordinances of baptism and the Lord's Supper a multisensory experience. At minimum, this experience is verbal, visual, and interactive. Blackwood's conclusion is that "The pastor who teaches in a multisensory form is not mimicking the culture; he is mimicking the Creator."[15]

Satterlee addresses the question of multisensory communication as it relates to those who are blind and their encounter with the Sunday morning sermon. He encourages pastors to preach to all the senses. Crucial to his argument is the role that all the senses play in Scripture. Satterlee points out that both the raising of Lazarus and Mary's anointing of Jesus involved the sense of smell. Preaching on Psalm 42:1 should involve taste and that which is thirst-quenching. Citing Jesus's cry, "My God, my God, why have you forsaken me?" Satterlee also emphasizes recognizing the way words would have sounded. Thus, a pastor, when preaching, ought to read Scripture in

---

[14] Yong, *The Bible, Disability, and the Church*, 74 (see chap. 4, n. 13).

[15] Rick Blackwood, *The Power of Multi-Sensory Preaching and Teaching: Increase Attention, Comprehension, and Retention* (Grand Rapids: Zondervan, 2008), 76–78.

a thoughtful manner. Satterlee argues that when the Bible is read in an engrossing manner, it can be both a proclamation of who God is as well as an experience of grace.[16]

Multisensory methodology extends beyond the sermon to issues of discipleship. Pastors ought to consider how they will provide those who have a disability the opportunity to demonstrate and continue to live out their profession of faith. The typical way in which faith is demonstrated is through a verbal expression of an internal belief. Benjamin T. Conner argues that we may need to rethink our one-size-fits-all approach to affirmations of the faith. He writes, "Are intellectual affirmations the most distinctive feature of participation in the Body of Christ? In what ways does such a perspective marginalize those with intellectual challenges?"[17] The spoken word and language comprehension can make outward expression of faith extremely difficult for those with disabilities. One way this issue can be overcome in discipleship is to encourage gestures of faith as evidence of a relationship with God.

What specifically do these gestures of faith toward God look like? Brett Webb-Mitchell writes, "A gesture is a fusion of mind, body, and spirit in Christ's one body by means of a physical act. Gestures are learned, practiced, and performed by members of Christ's body."[18] These actions, when practiced and performed by those who are disabled, help speak to what is taking place in their hearts and minds when words have failed.

Webb-Mitchell asserts that this type of bodily expression of faith is necessary for people with disabilities. He opines that education often begins with the body for people who have physical, emotional, behavioral, visual, auditory, or development disabilities. This education is focused on the intentional movement of the body in a way that reflects these gestures of

---

[16] Satterlee, "Learning to Picture God from Those Who Cannot See," 54.

[17] Benjamin T. Conner, *Amplifying Our Witness: Giving Voice to Adolescents with Developmental Disabilities* (Grand Rapids: Eerdmans, 2012), 94.

[18] Brett Webb-Mitchell, *Beyond Accessibility: Toward Full Inclusion of People with Disabilities in Faith Communities* (New York: Church Pub, 2010), 126.

faith. Webb-Mitchell articulates that these gestures are more than just "body language," pointing to an object or a response to a verbal cue. It is the Holy Spirit moving in these bodily gestures.[19]

Jeff and Kathi McNair present a similar idea but use the term "structure." These structures make up outward expressions of faith for those who, because of disability, have trouble expressing their faith. The McNairs state, "Faith is evidenced in their desire to have a Bible to carry, or requests for prayer for their bus driver or teacher, or having total access to anyone in the group independent of what they are doing."[20]

What do these structures look like in a faith formation or discipleship class? Is there a way for those with disabilities to demonstrate spiritual development and faith formation among their peers? The McNairs believe so and point to Psalm 1 as an example:

> In addition, we include opportunities to express how each person is growing in faith and how they practice faith on a weekly basis. Based on Psalm 1, class members share whether they "sat" (spent time in faith development through prayer, Bible reading, listening to Christian music, or watching Christian TV, movies, or videos), "stood" (stood up for what is right, resisted temptation, spoke about Jesus to someone) or "walked" (worked hard at their job, acted as a good citizen, attended church or Christian programs, or helped a person in need). Each person receives a card with three pictures on it that they raise to indicate what they have done the preceding week. Activities across the three areas are quite varied, often reflecting a person's current point of faith development.[21]

---

[19] Brett Webb-Mitchell, *Christly Gestures: Learning to Be Members of the Body of Christ* (Grand Rapids: Eerdmans, 2003), 90–93.

[20] Jeff McNair and Kathi McNair, "Faith Formation for Adults with Disability," in *Beyond Suffering: A Christian View on Disability Ministry*, ed. J. E. Tada and S. Bundy (Agoura Hills, CA: Joni and Friends Christian Institute on Disability, 2014), 473.

[21] McNair and McNair, 476.

Our churches are often programmed to the verbal expression of faith. This reality can have negative consequences for those with disabilities. One of the ways to compensate for this is to think "outside the box" and imagine what faith formation and spiritual growth looks like in nonverbal expressions. Structures or gestures of faith are ways those with a disability can express the development of faith in their lives as they are being discipled.

The challenge before the church in general, and church leaders specifically, is how to engage church members in a manner that effectively ministers to all, regardless of their physical or mental capabilities. Consideration of the full sensory experience ought to be a part of sermon preparation and discipleship if pastors are to believe themselves disability friendly and effective.

8

Jesus, the Synoptic Gospels, and Inclusive Leadership

Having examined selected texts by using a faithful hermeneutic, and with an eye toward disability, we can turn to Echols's five critical characteristics of inclusive leadership. These five characteristics will be used as a rubric to help understand if Jesus's ministry to the disabled fits Echols's framework of inclusive leadership.

According to Echols, inclusive leadership has the following characteristics:

1. Inclusive leadership brings the maximum number of individuals into participation.
2. Inclusive leadership empowers individuals to reach their full potential while pursuing the common good of the particular populace.
3. Inclusive leadership develops a culture that perpetuates the morality of the worth of the individual in such a way as to act as a preventive resistance against the ever-present possibility of despotism.

4. Inclusive leadership is intentional in the replication of today's leaders who model the above characteristics with a commitment to allow future leadership to emerge.

5. Inclusive leadership is manifested in the development of appropriate boundaries that maintain the integrity of the nature of the collective without marginalizing any of the populace.[1]

While Echols's essay does not touch on issues related to disability ministry or Jesus's healing miracles, these five characteristics can serve as a sufficient tool to analyze Jesus's ministry among the disabled. Was Jesus an inclusive leader? Specifically, did Jesus include those who were excluded and marginalized by society in a way that would allow for him to be recognized as an inclusive leader?

Jesus and Maximum Participation

The question of participation is one that is fairly simple to answer. Clearly, in each of these healing episodes Jesus was ministering to and healing someone who had been stigmatized and rejected by society. His healing drew them out of a place of exclusion and into a place of inclusion. The leper, the man with the withered hand, the hemorrhaging woman, the paralyzed man, and the blind man all found themselves ostracized by their culture. In most cases, their disability also came with the exclusionary label of "unclean." The sum total was tantamount to being declared untouchable.

Participation can also be seen in the way that "others" became involved in the healing process. In the healing of the paralyzed man, Jesus saw "their faith" as opposed to "his faith" (Mark 2:5). The implication of the plural *their* is a demonstration of Jesus's choice to involve others in the healing of the paralyzed man. He was recognizing and validating what they brought to the healing encounter. It was not simply the paralyzed man who held a

---

[1] Echols, "Transformational/Servant Leadership," 88–91 (see chap. 1, n. 15).

certain belief and hope in Jesus. Rather, it was the paralyzed man and those who brought him to Jesus.

These healing stories also demonstrate the way Jesus tried to involve those who opposed him as well. When he directed the question about forgiveness or healing to the religious leaders, it was to involve them in what was about to take place. He was revealing to them something of himself in hopes that they would connect what they knew about the one who was to be the Messiah to what they were witnessing. The same was also true with the way Jesus engaged the religious leaders in the healing of the man with a withered hand. By asking them to compare the value of a sheep to the value of a human being, they were participants in the eventual healing. While these men choose to be silent, they were not excluded from the miracle. Indeed, it was their silence that only added to their participation in the healing of the man with the withered hand. Their silence spoke volumes and clearly articulated their position against Jesus and the man with the withered hand.

In the restoration of sight to blind Bartimaeus, Jesus involved a crowd that was originally guilty of excluding the beggar. It was Jesus's concern for Bartimaeus, and the mercy he was more than willing to show him, that moved the crowd from marginalization to participation. The crowd shifted from telling Bartimaeus "be quiet" to "cheer up." This change in perspective had everything to do with Jesus's impact on the situation. Jesus could have walked over to Bartimaeus instead of telling the crowd to bring him to him. Yet, Jesus turned the crowd from a group of spectators into engaged participants.

When considering the healing of the hemorrhaging woman, Jesus chose to use her as a model of faith to encourage and develop the faith of Jairus. Yet, the participatory nature of Jesus's inclusion in this story goes further than just that one moment on the road. It also extended to his selection of Peter, James, John, and the young girl's parents. Jesus specifically selected this group to be participants with a front row seat to this raising of Jairus's daughter. Jesus wanted each of them to participate in this miracle by watching him reveal his power over death. It could be assumed that even in the way Jesus responded to the negative reactions of Jairus's servants and the mourners he was challenging them to believe and participate as well.

Finally, when Jesus healed the leper, he told the man to go to show himself to the priest "as a testimony to them" (Matt 8:4). Once again, Jesus was drawing others into the participation of his healing miracle. For Jesus, the priest's acceptance of the prescribed sacrifice served as a testimony to Jesus's nature and ministry. However, it also allowed the priests, by way of sacrifice, to participate in the healing by admitting the once-leprous man back into the community. The priest would participate in this healing by pronouncing the man healed and affirming his access into the religious and social community.

Each of these episodes, by way of both the main character and the supporting characters, give evidence to Jesus's inclusive leadership. He purposefully chose to involve others in these miracles so that they too could either accept or reject him.

Jesus and Individual Empowerment

Each of these healing episodes demonstrates Jesus's empowerment of the individual because their healing removed a societal stigmatization. The hemorrhaging woman was no longer defined by her bleeding. The man with the withered hand was no longer looked at distrustfully because he exclusively used his left hand. The paralyzed man was no longer confined to his own home or dependent on his friends for assistance. Bartimaeus was no longer a blind beggar who relied on the generosity of his community for survival. The leper near Gennesaret need not shout "Unclean!" to warn people to stay away. At a fundamental level, the disabilities that hindered them were removed, and they were able to overcome the marginalization of society. What Jesus did for each of them was not something they could have ever accomplished on their own.

However, leaving this characteristic of inclusive leadership at the level of physical healing does an injustice to these miracles. It misses the way Jesus's physical healings led to spiritual healings as well. In other words, in these stories Jesus's healings were often more about wholeness than just removing a disability. The hemorrhaging woman and Bartimaeus, because of their faith, were made both physically and spiritually well.

The challenge for church leaders that comes with this characteristic of inclusive leadership is to emphasize empowerment through wholeness despite a disability. The church leader must be able to articulate the reality of the wholeness that comes through a relationship with Jesus Christ. A blind parishioner should not look at the story of Bartimaeus and believe that Bartimaeus's joy will always be elusive because he or she will never know what it is like to receive sight. Consequently, a pastor should seek to develop a robust theology of brokenness within his congregation. This theology will help church members understand that brokenness is a characteristic that has impacted every human being since the fall of mankind in Genesis 3. When the fundamental brokenness of every person is taught and recognized by a congregation, it will help eliminate a false dichotomy between those who are whole and those who need healing. Instead, the congregation will recognize that everyone is broken and in need of healing and wholeness.

Jesus and the Worth of the Individual

In much the same way that the healings performed by Jesus empowered individuals, they also exhibited the worth of those who were healed. His interaction with the disabled ran counter to a society that viewed each of their disabilities in a negative light. Whether it was a serious skin disease, blindness, paralysis, or a deformity of some variety, each of these issues would have created a question of worth or value in biblical culture. This issue is most highlighted by Jesus's confrontation with the religious leaders. When he questioned the religious leaders about rescuing sheep on the Sabbath, he was using a lesser-to-greater argument to establish the value of human life. His question to the religious leaders was asking them to evaluate what they believed had more worth—one sheep or one human being. Their silence in answering his question was what drew both the anger and compassion of Jesus. While these leaders would acknowledge that human beings were created in the image of God, they would not practically apply that belief to a man with a withered hand.

In Jesus's healing of the woman with the issue of blood, he used the name *daughter* to address her (Matt 9:22). This intimate and friendly address expressed personal and familial value to one who was a societal outcast because of her affliction. It is doubtful that the expression *daughter* was used all that frequently as a means of addressing her. Yet, this is how Jesus viewed her. While others saw her as unclean, Jesus viewed her as family, as his daughter. Thus, her value and worth was not just as a human being but as a much-loved family member.

Jesus also conveyed the worth of an individual through the ways compassion was either stated or shown in these healing stories. On two occasions, the healing of blind Bartimaeus and in the curing of the leper, Jesus was said to have been moved with compassion. Rather than seeing these two men as object of ridicule, he saw their divine worth. In this empathy, he was stirred to action. He was moved to act on their behalf. This compassion was further evidenced by Jesus's willingness to touch leprous skin or seeping blind eyes. For both men, human contact was probably not something freely given. Fear and the ever-present reality of being labeled unclean would have caused most of society to avoid contact with these men. Christ, in divine compassion, feared neither disease nor disability. Instead, he touched both men to heal them. In so doing, he communicated a resounding message to the leper, blind Bartimaeus, and anyone else willing to listen. Jesus's touch proclaims that the worth and value of a human being is not advanced or diminished based on ability or disability.

Jesus and the Replication of Inclusive Leaders

Did Jesus reproduce inclusive leaders? In other words, were his followers as inclusive as he was, once they were tasked with taking the gospel to the world? While none of these stories take place after Jesus's ascension, the question posed is still one that can be considered: Were Jesus's disciples so transformed by his inclusive ministry that they too sought to be inclusive?

The book of Acts tells of occasions where Jesus's inclusive approach clearly rubbed off on the disciples. Two incidents are worth commenting on. The first incident is the healing of the lame man in Acts 3:1–10. Peter and John engaged a man lame from birth who was begging outside of the temple complex. Similar to Jesus, Peter and John stopped, asked the man to look at them, and then took him by the right hand and helped him up. Each of these actions was a reflection of Christ. The two apostles stopped and gave the lame beggar an audience at his request for help. They did not walk quickly by him or avoid him as others may have done. Instead, they offered him dignity by honoring his humanity. They asked him to look at them. This request speaks to the level of personal engagement. With this request, the two apostles were personally investing in this man.

Where others may have looked on this man with disgust, these two men looked toward him with compassion. They wanted him to see divine compassion rather than human repulsion. Then, after invoking the name and power of Jesus Christ, they touched him. In much the same way as their master, they extended a hand of inclusion and helped him to his feet. A look of compassion and a hand of inclusion lead to celebration in the temple. This man was wholly restored into the community of faith. This interaction shows just how much Peter and John learned from Jesus when it came to disabilities and inclusion.

A second incident from Acts also demonstrates just how much the apostles gleaned from Jesus with regard to inclusion. The end of Acts 7 features the introduction of a man named Saul. As Acts 8 and 9 unfold, Saul goes from persecutor of the church to blinded follower of God. After his Damascus Road conversion experience, he was introduced to a man named Ananias. When he met Saul, he healed Saul's blindness and baptized him. Acts 9:19 notes that Saul remained with the disciples in Damascus for some time. Once again, this episode contains evidence of the inclusive ministry of Jesus Christ. Ananias befriends, shows compassion, and offers healing to the one-time enemy of the church. He also extends to him the ordinance of baptism. Further, Saul's conversion results in acceptance and integration into the community of faith. Each one of these elements resembles something from Jesus's meaningful and purposeful ministry of inclusion.

Jesus and Boundary Development

The issue of boundary development takes place on two fronts for Jesus. First, he must navigate the Torah and the Jewish Levitical laws. Much has been written and continues to be written on this front. Time and space do not permit a recollection of the many nuances that make up the scholarly discussion on Jesus and the Jewish boundaries of his culture. Second, Jesus's teachings and actions reveal a new kind of boundary for the citizens of the new kingdom. These boundary markers are reflected in teachings like the Sermon on the Mount. In this sermon, Jesus uses the comparison technique of "you've heard it said . . . but I say . . ." as a means of highlighting where these new boundary markers are.

Perhaps the most concise description of these new inclusionary boundaries was expressed by Jesus in Matt 22:36–40 and Mark 12:28–31 where he was questioned on the greatest commandment. In response to this question, Jesus says, "'Love the Lord your God with all your heart and with all your soul and with all your mind.' . . . The second is like it: 'Love your neighbor as yourself'" (Matt 22:37, 39 NIV). This simple "love God and love others" statement frames the way that Jesus engaged those who were marginalized and stigmatized by his culture. He saw touching a leper or healing a man on a Sabbath as representing these two commands. This representation was over and against the way other Jewish legal rules were interpreted and kept. Of priority was not the day or the disability but the image of God reflected in these two human beings. Thus, the only thing to do was exhibit the compassion and mercy and God.

The same could also be said for Jesus's interaction with the hemorrhaging woman, a dead child, a paralyzed man, or a blind beggar. In his compassion and willingness to engage each of these people, Jesus showed what love for God and love for others looked like. Disability was not a reason to avoid or marginalize human beings who were important image-bearers. Indeed, it was Jesus's ability to summarize so succinctly and to practice the law through these two boundaries that frustrated his opponents. When their frustration turned to questions, it often resulted in silence. Jesus's ability to explain his actions based on his love for his Father and his love for others often left them bewildered and angered. It was this same commitment to love God and love others that would routinely get the apostles in trouble as well.

These selected healing episodes in the Synoptic Gospels capture the way Jesus sought to embrace those who were marginalized and cast aside by society. In these interactions, he revealed the intrinsic value and worth of every human being as he empowered them through his compassion for them. As he established the boundary lines for the new kingdom, he sought to include any who would follow him. Inclusion was not just for those whose immediate interaction was friendly. Further, these inclusive interactions became teachable moments for his disciples. Once Jesus had ascended to heaven, these men were able to be inclusive leaders themselves. Their three years of following Jesus had given them sufficient preparation to reach out and include the marginalized wherever they were found.

9

Jesus and the Disabled in John's Gospel

(John 5:1–18)

In 2 Sam 5:6–12, King David set his eyes on Jerusalem as the capital city of Israel. However, the town was already occupied by the Jebusites. As he and his men prepared to lay siege to the city, they were taunted by these Jebusites, who believed that they had built a city so well fortified that it was impenetrable. They mocked David and his men by telling them that even the blind and lame could protect their city. When David captured the city and established it as the "City of David," he boldly proclaimed that the lame and the blind will never enter the "house" (CSB). Scholars debate the meaning of this statement as well as David's statement about hating the lame and blind. However, Jewish writing indicates that the exclusion of the disabled from the temple finds its roots in this passage.[1]

---

[1] See Saul M. Olyan "Anyone Blind or Lame Shall Not Enter the House: On the Interpretation of 2 Samuel 5:8b," in *Catholic Biblical Quarterly* 60, no. 2 (April 1998): 218–27.

As the pages of Scripture move from the Old Testament to the New Testament and the characters in the story shift from David to Jesus, the lame and the blind in Jerusalem form an ironic connection between these two men. In Jesus's Jerusalem healing ministry, he only heals two men. He heals a lame man gathered around the pool at Bethesda, and he heals a man born blind. Thus, the lame and blind of Jerusalem figure prominently in both the lives of David and Jesus.

While this connection is interesting, can more be understood about Jesus's healing of the man born blind in John 9 and the lame man in John 5? More specifically, and as it relates to this biblical investigation, is it possible to discern if Jesus was an inclusive leader based on his interactions with these two disabled men?

Healing of Lame Man at Bethesda (John 5:1–18)

John 5 describes how Jesus made his way to Jerusalem to observe one of the Jewish feasts. While there, Jesus made his way to the pool of Bethesda. This place was near the Sheep Gate, a place where the lame, blind, and paralyzed gathered because they believed the nearby pool had some healing properties. When the water moved, the first one in would be healed of their ailment. Jesus found out about a man who had been disabled for thirty-eight years and made his way over to where he was laying. Jesus asked him a question: "Do you want to get well?" The man's response was not a "yes" or a "no." Rather, he explained why he could not get well. He did not have someone to take him to the water once it stirred. When he tried to get there, someone else was quicker and got in before him. After hearing this, Jesus told the man to get up, pick up his mat, and walk. The man was instantly made well. He got up, picked up his mat, and walked away. Jesus slipped into the crowd and disappeared from sight.

While the healed man was walking away, one of the Jewish leaders confronted him about breaking the Sabbath. He told the man it was illegal to carry his mat on the Sabbath. The now-healed man responded by saying that the one who healed him told him to do it. When questioned further, he admitted he did not know who his healer was. Later, Jesus ran into the man in the temple complex. Jesus told him to stop sinning so that something worse would not happen to him. The healed man found the religious leaders and told them it was Jesus who had healed him. It was because of Jesus's healing on the Sabbath that the religious leaders began persecuting Jesus. However, Jesus responded by telling them that his Father was still working on the Sabbath, so he would work also.

Examining this story through a literary lens that focuses on Jesus's encounter with the disabled reveals three elements that need investigation: the debilitating presence of disability, the actions of Jesus, and the absence of faith. Each of these elements shape the direction of the story. The actions of Jesus and the disabled man, as well as the way they interact with each other, reveal much about Jesus's approach to those who have a disability. These interactions also reveal something of the self-perception that can plague those with a disability.

The Debilitating Presence of Disability

John's recollection of the lame man in this event includes details that point to just how this man's disability had impacted him. One of the most obvious descriptions of his disability is the number of years he was disabled. The text says he was disabled for thirty-eight years. The length of the man's illness helps set the stage for understanding the full scope of his disability. Keener notes three things with regard to this man's disability. First, the duration of the man's disability was longer than most people in ancient times lived. Second, ancient reports of healings often provided the length of the disability to affirm the greatness of the healer. Third, thirty-eight years is akin to the number of years Israel wandered in the wilderness. Keener does not specify whether he thinks there is something symbolic or allegorical being made by this last point. Thus, he does not affirm or deny how the early church fathers understood the numeric allegory in this healing story.[2] Köstenberger affirms Keener's first point by stating that, given the length of the disability and the average life expectancy of the men in antiquity, this man had his disability longer than most men lived.[3]

Gerald L. Borchert seems to argue for some hyperbolic symbolism or allegory to the years of the man's disability and the years of Israel's desert wanderings. He considers the man's disability experience as feeling like a "wilderness of abandonment for what seemed to have been eternity." This reality, according to Borchert, is the same "eternity" feeling the Israelites had to have experienced as they wandered from Kadesh to the brook Zered.[4]

D. A. Carson asserts that there is no reason to believe the man had lived at the pool for thirty-eight years. Instead, he imagines that, for the past thirty-eight years, the man was brought to the pool whenever it was assumed the water was likely to stir.[5] While Carson's suggestion makes sense at first blush, it does not fit neatly into the disabled man's rationale for his inability to be healed by the water. One would presume that if this man had friends or loved ones who cared enough to bring him to the pool, they would stay around and help him get into the pool when the water stirred. Rodney A. Whitacre offers probably the most astute observation between Carson's suggestion and the healing potential of the pool. Whitacre notes that the man had frequented the pool for thirty-eight years and not been healed. Thus, he must have missed the stirring of the water and its supposed healing properties on a number of occasions.[6]

Given this information, it is wise not to miss this character descriptor. The man has been disabled for quite some time. In fact, his disability is extraordinary in length since its duration is longer than most men lived during his day.

---

[2] Keener, *IVP Bible Background Commentary* 262 (see chap. 5, n. 14).

[3] Andreas J. Köstenberger, *John*, Baker Exegetical Commentary on the New Testament (Grand Rapids: Baker Academic, 2004), 179.

[4] Gerald L. Borchert, *John 1–11*, New American Commentary, vol. 25a (Nashville: B&H, 1996), 232.

[5] D. A. Carson, *The Gospel According to John* (Grand Rapids: Eerdmans, 1991), 243.

[6] Rodney A. Whitacre, *John*, IVP New Testament Commentary Series, vol. 4 (Downers Grove, IL: InterVarsity, 1999), 119.

While the passage does not specify that he was lame from birth, it is entirely conceivable that he had spent the majority of his life as a lame man. Borchert's "feeling of eternity" claim may seem anecdotal, but it does present the reality of how this man must have felt. For most, if not all, of his life, he was unable to use his legs. The impact of this disability in a culture that lacked our modern accessibility technology cannot be understated. His inability to walk and the other complications that would have come with this paralysis could have contributed to the feeling that Borchert is speculatively presenting.

The duration of the illness is only one factor to consider in the debilitating presence of the disability. A second consideration is the overall physical condition of a lame man during that period of history. Citing the personal experience of wheelchair-bound scholar Dwight Peterson, Gary M. Burge vividly estimates what it might look like to encounter this man:

> The challenges of a paraplegic in the twenty-first century (which are considerable) pale by comparison with a person in the first century. Problems of mobility and livelihood and social isolation just begin the list. Consider the problem of personal hygiene. . . . Paraplegics frequently do not have bowel and bladder control. Taking these issues together we can build a portrait of this man's life: People moved him from place to place unless he crawled; most of his income came from begging or from the charity of friends and family; and if he did not have bladder or bowel control, his hygiene problem would have been enormous. People stayed away from him. His hands (used for mobility) were rough and torn from the streets.[7]

Burge's description is one of physical, mental, and social misery. The totality of this man's condition can easily be overlooked by inadvertently reading modern disability access into this story. However, the physical, mental, and social problems that plagued the disabled in antiquity were exacerbated by the lack of accessibility and technology.

---

[7] Gary M. Burge, *John*, NIV Application Commentary (Grand Rapids: Zondervan, 2000), 183.

The wounds that would have marred this man go deeper than physical wounds. His condition would have exposed him to psychological and emotional wounds inflicted by society. David W. Anderson places these wounds in four categories. The crippled man had suffered status, rejection, personal, and material/experiential wounds. The status wounds inflicted on the lame man included being assigned a lower social status and seen as a deviant. This status wound is reflected by his namelessness in the text. Rejection wounds are characterized by abandonment and the burden disability places on society. For the lame man, these rejection wounds could be found in his removal from society and assignment around a pool where he was left alone, without the support of family or friends. Personal wounds relate to the loss of real and meaningful relationships, as well as the perception of being less than human. The paralyzed man lacked both family and friends. Additionally, he had not learned a skill or trade. He contributed nothing to his sociocultural world and had no value because of this. He was simply a disabled man. Finally, the crippled man suffered material and/or experiential wounds. These wounds were related to the separation from a physical environment, physical and material poverty, as well as exploitation. John's description of this man reinforces his connection to one group of people. He was part of the disabled community who gathered around a pool in hopes of healing. Other than his bed, he had no personal possessions.[8]

Draycott, citing the work of Emma-Jayne Graham, argues that there was a "sliding scale of physical impairment," where those with physical impairments were treated differently from more able-bodied individuals in ancient Greek and Roman cultures. This evaluation resulted in those with disabilities being considered "suitable for public mockery and humiliation."[9]

---

[8] David W. Anderson, *Reaching Out and Bringing In: Ministry to and with Persons with Disabilities* (Bloomington, IN: WestBow, 2013), 84.

[9] Jane Draycott, "Reconstructing the Lived Experience of Disability in Antiquity: A Case Study from Roman Egypt," *Greece & Rome* 62, no. 2 (October 2015): 201, https://doi.org/10.1017/S0017383515000066.

When consideration is given to each of these areas, we can begin to get a clearer picture of the lame man. He was a man who had been in this condition for a considerable length of time. In fact, he had a disability longer than most men live. His physical condition was one that was unattractive and would cause people to avoid him rather than socialize with him. This circumstance resulted in numerous social wounds that were represented throughout John's recount of this healing event. All these elements contribute to an image of a man whose disability was so profound that it impacted him physically, socially, and mentally. It is not very hard to imagine a man who has given up all hope because of his circumstance.

David Lee Jones imagines the crippled man "may feel frustrated, discouraged, exhausted, embarrassed, ashamed, empty, and even worthless" because of his thirty-eight years of disability. Jones believes it is entirely possible "that the paralytic man never directly answers Jesus's question because his hopelessness stifles his own capacity to imagine healing aside from his single-minded focus on getting into the pool." He could only envision one way to be made well, and he had no potential to get to the pool first.[10] Carson views John as describing this man in "dour hues." Consequently, his response to Jesus is very much "the crotchety grumblings of an old and not perceptive man." This man had no desire in answering what he perceived to be a stupid question.[11] Merrill C. Tenney also sees the man's perceived hopelessness reflected in his answer to Jesus about being healed. Tenney believes Jesus was searching the man's heart and asked a question that should be understood as, "Have you the will to be cured?" The question and his subsequent answer reflect the heart of man who is both paralyzed of body and paralyzed of will.[12]

---

[10] David Lee Jones, "A Pastoral Model for Caring for Persons with Diminished Hope," *Pastoral Psychology* 58, no. 5–6 (December 2009): 644.

[11] Carson, *Gospel According to John*, 244.

[12] Merrill C. Tenney, *John: The Gospel of Belief* (Grand Rapids: Eerdmans, 1997), 105.

This hopelessness is something that should not be missed when it comes to disability. It is easy for those with a disability to succumb to hopelessness. When they view their physical ailment alongside the mental and social wounds they have experienced, it becomes easy for a disabled individual to look at life in a forlorn and miserable manner. J. I. Packer and Carolyn Nystrom understand the connection between hope and life:

> The death of hope has a killing effect on human minds and hearts. While there's life there's hope, we say, but the deeper truth is that only while there's hope is there life. Take away hope, and life, with all its fascinating variety of opportunities and experiences, reduces to mere existence—uninteresting, ungratifying, bleak, drab and repellent, a burden and a pain.[13]

This forlorn condition is exactly where the lame man in John 5 can be found. He had reached a state of hopelessness. Jesus's question only served to confirm this. He could not figure any way that he would ever be well. This hopelessness is where many who have a disability can find themselves as well. Their hopes and dreams have all been crushed by the reality of their life. They cannot imagine a life that looks any different or better than what they are presently experiencing. Consequently, one of the most important things church leadership and church members can do for the disabled is to help them hope and dream again. A church that provides healing for the mental and social wounds of disability is an emotionally restorative environment for the disabled. In this atmosphere, they will come to find the joy and hope they thought had been lost.

The Actions of Jesus in John 5:1–17

If the question were asked, "What did Jesus do in John 5:1–17?" the answer given would be something like, "He healed a lame man." On the

---

[13] J. I. Packer and Carolyn Nystrom, *Never beyond Hope: How God Touches & Uses Imperfect People* (Downers Grove, IL: InterVarsity, 2000), 9–10.

surface, that is a correct answer. However, he did so much more along the way to this healing. Two points of actions should be noted. First, Jesus's appearance at the pool of Bethesda is significant. Second, the action of Jesus to purposefully seek out this lame man should also be observed. Considering these actions helps us understand something of Jesus's concern for the disabled.

First, Jesus made an appearance at a place that many of his religious contemporaries would not frequent. Köstenberger views the descriptive detail of the Sheep Gate as referencing a small opening located near the temple where sheep were cleaned before they were brought into the temple complex. Additionally, this was also the place where the city's disabled were brought for the possibility of healing in the pool. These two factors would cause the societal elite and those desiring to stay ritually pure to avoid this area. However, Köstenberger notes, neither of these two factors kept Jesus away.[14]

Further complicating matters for Jesus, Keener believes that religious authorities would have viewed a healing pool as something similar to the healing pools of the Greek cults like Asclepius. Consequently, they would have frowned upon the site and what it connoted.[15] Accordingly, it would be safe to assume that, for religious reasons, the Jewish leaders would have avoided an area like the pool at Bethesda.

Borchert points out that Jesus's attendance around the pool of Bethesda reminds us of where Jesus would spend time when he was in Jerusalem. He did not visit elite hostels or focus on an exclusive temple ministry. He did not purposefully seek out the rich, famous, or politically powerful when he was in that city. Instead, Jesus single-mindedly determined to meet with those in need. He visited with those whom the societal elite would label as the dregs of culture. While they would not want to walk among the disabled and suffering, Jesus made a point to do just that. The religious leaders may have been uncomfortable in that type of situation. The potential violation

---

[14] Köstenberger, *John*, 178.
[15] Keener, *IVP Bible Background Commentary*, 262 (see chap. 5, n. 14).

of the purity rules would have been a deterrent. However, neither the disabled individuals nor the purity rituals were constraining for Jesus.[16]

An interesting understanding of this pool is proposed by Charles R. Swindoll. He argues that the pool of Bethesda had a strong resemblance to the Greek *asklēpieion,* or religious sanitarium. If it was indeed Greek in design, then it would have been dedicated to Asclepius, a Greek god known as a gentle healer. He also believes it is located within close proximity to Herod's temple. Swindoll notes that if this was the case, then Jesus went to a pagan sanitarium to find this lame man. Thus, he was going into a place no Pharisee or religious leader would ever want to go. Indeed, the religious leaders would have probably rebuked anyone who did find their way into a pagan sanitarium.[17]

This view is also proposed by Eli Lizorkin-Eyzenberg of the Israel Institute of Biblical Studies. He speculates that the pool at Bethesda was an amalgamation of Greco-Roman and Jewish ideas. Thus, it was not a full Jewish pool like the pool at Siloam was. This mixture of ideas would be the reason Jesus did not tell the lame man at Bethesda to bathe in this pool, while he instructs the blind man in John 9 to bathe in the pool at Siloam. Additionally, he suggests that those who, like the lame man, have gathered around the pool of Bethesda have given up seeking help from Israel's God and have turned to the Greco-Roman god Asclepius for healing.[18]

The proposition that the pool at Bethesda was a syncretistic mix of Greco-Roman and Jewish beliefs is an interesting one. Research reveals that, at best, it is the minority opinion. However, even if it were so, it does not change the fact that Jesus made an appearance at a place no religious leader of his time would have visited. Either the ritual impurity of the pool or the theological underpinning of the pool would have caused the Pharisees and

---

[16] Borchert, *John 1–11*, 231–32.

[17] Charles R. Swindoll, *Insights on John*, Swindoll's New Testament Insights (Grand Rapids: Zondervan, 2010), 107–8.

[18] Eli Lizorkin-Eyzenberg, "The Pool of Bethesda as a Healing Center of Asclepius," *Israel Institute of Biblical Studies* (blog), December 1, 2014, https://blog.israelbiblicalstudies.com/jewish-studies/bethesda-pool-jerusalem-shrine-asclepius/.

religious leaders to stay away from that location. Yet, Jesus is drawn to a pool that is populated by those who have been relegated to the outside by their culture and religious community.

This image is one that Christians ought to frame in their mind. Jesus willingly and purposefully went to the places that teemed with the marginalized and stigmatized of culture. He could be found in the places that others would not go. He did not let fear or popular opinion dictate the direction of his ministry. For contemporary churches, there are programmatic implications due to Jesus's attendance at Bethesda. Churches can be guilty of planning and instituting programs based on popular opinion rather than community need. Thus, outreach becomes more a matter of what is new and popular in church ministry rather than attending to the needs of those who find themselves on the outside of most societal groups. A church that prioritizes an inward-focused niche program over and against implementing a Celebrate Recovery–type program may be guilty of such neglect.[19] Culpability is enlarged if the purpose of this prioritization reflects a fear of how a program like Celebrate Recovery might alter the human dynamic of the church.

The second action of Jesus that requires further observation is his discerning of the needs of the lame man. The issue centers on how Jesus "saw" and "knew" the paralyzed man was there at the pool. More specifically, the question is, "How did Jesus know what he knew about this man?" Hendriksen concludes that there are three possible answers to this question. First, Jesus received the information through human discussion. Second, Jesus received this information because God the Father revealed it directly to him. In the third option, Jesus's divine nature is responsible for bringing this to the attention of Jesus's human nature. Hendriksen admits that, with this third option, the transformation of information would occur through a process we do not understand.[20]

---

[19] Celebrate Recovery is a Christ-centered, 12-step program for those who struggle with addictions or overcoming hurts. See https://www.celebraterecovery.com/.

[20] William Hendriksen, *Exposition of the Gospel According to John*, Baker New Testament Commentary (Grand Rapids: Baker, 1953), 1:192.

Carson structures these three possibilities by intimating that Jesus either found out about the paralyzed man's condition through diligent inquiry, or this healing episode demonstrates Jesus's sovereign initiative. Carson believes this man was picked out for healing by Jesus. As such, it differs from other healings such as the paralytic in Mark 2:1–12, who came to Jesus for healing through an opened roof.[21] Köstenberger also notes that there is no clarity as to how Jesus "saw" and "knew" the condition of the lame man. He understands that the language could connote either knowledge gained supernaturally or knowledge gained through investigation. He also speculates that Jesus's conversation with the paralyzed man could have originated out of his request for alms.[22] Given this speculation, if it was simply through inquiry, what is missing in the text pertains to the first part of the conversation that creates the question of healing proposed by Jesus.

Tenney highlights the supernatural knowledge Jesus has with regard to this man and his paralysis. For him, this is crucial to seeing what takes place as coming by the direct volition of Jesus. Tenney asserts that this man was selected by Jesus among all the other disabled individuals around the pool. This selection was in keeping with Jesus's desire to heal those whose helplessness was evident in both their body and spirit.[23]

To the contrary, Morris would seem to favor a more talkative and less direct Jesus, who learned of this man and his disability through the process of an ongoing conversation. Morris does indeed recognize both the divine and natural options with respect to Jesus's knowledge of the lame man. However, he seems to lean toward the possibility that Jesus learned of the man's condition by conversation with the man or another individual.[24]

Murray J. Harris agrees that both the natural and divine options are possibilities. However, he highlights the emotion of the moment. He believes

---

[21] Carson, *Gospel According to John*, 243.

[22] Köstenberger, *John*, 180.

[23] Tenney, *John*, 105.

[24] Leon Morris, *The Gospel According to John*, rev. ed, New International Commentary on the New Testament (Grand Rapids: Eerdmans, 1995), 269.

that the original language of this passage underscores that Jesus saw the man lying there in a pitiful condition and learned how long he had been in that state.[25] Harris is not the only one to see the compassion of Jesus in this encounter. Hendriksen also picks up on the emotion of the passage by suggesting that when Jesus saw the man, he did so through the eyes of sympathy because he knew the duration of the man's condition.[26]

Regardless of how one views Jesus's knowledge in this encounter, what is clear is his purposeful and compassionate engagement with the disabled man. This example should push church leaders to do the same. Pastors should think through the ways they are engaged with the disabled community. This purposeful interaction is respectful and thoughtful. Anderson argues that Jesus interacts with the paralyzed man in a respectful manner. The question Jesus asks is designed to allow the man to express his needs and wants. This approach stands counter to Jesus simply acting on the healing he can safely assume the man wants. This question opens a conversation and allows the man to express his perspective. In so doing, Jesus's encounter is a respectful one.[27]

Jesus's interaction with the crippled man was also a thoughtful interaction. Jesus asked a question and then listened to the man's response. His question was designed to allow the man to enter into a conversation with Jesus. In this conversation, Jesus participated through both talking and listening. This duality is an important consideration for disability ministries. More specifically, measuring the words of this dialogue reveals that Jesus did more listening than talking.

Amy Fenton Lee makes the point that in disability ministries it is important to talk less and listen more. She makes this argument when discussing how to demonstrate affection to parents who have received a disability diagnosis for a child. She believes that making this commitment to talk less and

---

[25] Murray J. Harris, *John*, Exegetical Guide to the Greek New Testament (Nashville: B&H Academic, 2015), 105.

[26] Hendriksen, *Exposition of the Gospel According to John*, 1:191.

[27] Anderson, *Reaching Out and Bringing In*, 88.

listen more creates a safe space for the expression of authentic feelings.[28] Jesus's encounter with the paralyzed man is one that models this safe space. His question and his subsequent commitment to listening creates an atmosphere in which the man feels free to express himself in an open and honest manner. This environment is clearly evidenced through the way the lame man feels free to express his rationale for the impossibility of his healing.

Purposeful and thoughtful engagement of those who are disabled was something modeled by Jesus Christ. He sought out this lame man among the crowd gathered around the pool. When he approached him, he asked a simple question that opened an avenue of communication. He followed it up by listening to the man's honest response. Further, he kept the safe space open in how he responded to the man. Jesus did not chastise the man for not recognizing him. He did not castigate him for giving a rationale that seemed excuse laden. In doing so, Jesus showed the disabled man utmost respect. Purposeful and thoughtful engagement is still one of the best ways that pastors and church leaders can connect with the disabled community today.

The Absence of Faith in John 5:1–17

One of the most startling factors in this healing miracle of Jesus is that this encounter is devoid of faith throughout the entirety of the narrative. The man by the pool never expressed faith in Jesus before he was healed. Neither did he express faith in Jesus after the healing when he was confronted by his healer once again. In fact, it appears his only response to Jesus's work in his life was to place blame on Jesus for the charge of Sabbath violation he received from the religious leaders. Further, the man was more than willing to implicate Jesus in a subsequent conversation with the religious leaders. Given the way John records the growing animosity between Jesus and the

---

[28] Amy Fenton Lee, *Leading a Special Needs Ministry* (Nashville: B&H, 2016), 10–11.

religious leaders, the man's actions were more in keeping with betrayal than thankfulness.

At two points, the lame man had the opportunity to express faith in Christ and he failed to do so. The first opportunity to demonstrate faith was immediately after the healing had taken place. The second was when Jesus found him in the temple and challenged him to stop sinning. Scholars appear to be more sympathetic to the man's lack of faith in his first encounter with Jesus. Cornelis Bennema does not hold the lame man responsible for not knowing who Jesus is either before or after the healing. The man's complaint about his situation was recognition that he did not know who Jesus was and his ability to heal. His inability to learn Jesus's name after the healing has more to do with the way Jesus left the scene around the pool than the passivity of the once-lame man. However, Bennema does suggest that the man's lack of faith is revealed in his inability to give testimony to Jesus in a critical situation. In this, he is unlike the Samaritan woman in John 4 and the blind man in John 9.[29]

Jacobus Kok argues that John links knowledge and faith together in his Gospel. This linkage means that those who do not know Jesus are the very ones who both do not believe and do not know the Father. They do not know eternal life and live in spiritual death. For Kok, the lame man of John 5 is an example of this linkage.[30] This connection, as Kok develops it, suggests that the man's lack of faith is evident before the healing, when the man was confronted by the religious leaders for carrying his mat on the Sabbath, and then finally when Jesus admonished him in the temple. In this temple scene, the once-lame man simply knew Jesus as a healer and reported him as such to the religious leaders.

---

[29] Cornelis Bennema, *Encountering Jesus: Character Studies in the Gospel of John*, 2nd ed. (Minneapolis: Fortress, 2014), 188–91.

[30] Jacobus (Kobus) Kok, *New Perspectives on Healing, Restoration, and Reconciliation in John's Gospel*, Biblical Interpretation Series, vol. 149 (Leiden, NL: Brill, 2017), 126.

The man's indifferent reaction is detailed by Craig R. Koester where he determines that the man was unresponsive to what he heard from Jesus. This apathy is evident both right after the healing and then later when he was confronted in the temple. Thus, this man's lack of faith stands in contrast to the faith of the official whose son was healed in John 4:46–54. Koester points out that "simply seeing or experiencing a miracle is no guarantee of faith."[31] This lame man was much like the crowds in John 2:23–25, who did not believe even though they had seen the miraculous.[32]

The once-lame man's lack of faith was what leads Jesus to press him to sin no more for fear of something worse happening to him. Some scholars see this statement by Jesus as highlighting the man's disability as a result of a particular sin. This interpretation taken by Whitacre when he asserts a clear connection between the sin of this man and his illness. However, he cautions against making assumptions in similar cases since the blindness of the man in John 9 is not connected to sin.[33] Carson believes that the man's disability was indeed the result of a particular sin. He notes that syntactically Jesus's two statements, "stop sinning" and "something worse may happen to you" are connected to each other. Thus, his previous disability was the result of a sin that he must not repeat. Carson speculates that if his interpretation is correct, "the syntax of *stop sinning* is chosen to stress urgency. The *something worse* must be final judgment."[34]

Carson provides one of the most thorough analyses of the possible meanings of these two statements before coming to his conclusion. However, the one detail missing from his arguments is a consideration of the length of the man's illness and the life expectancy of a man during this time period. If Carson (and Whitacre, for that matter) is correct, this man's thirty-eight years of disability are the result of a sin committed very early on in his life.

---

[31] Craig R. Koester, "Hearing, Seeing, and Believing in the Gospel of John," *Biblica* 70, no. 3 (1989): 338.

[32] Koester, 337–38.

[33] Whitacre, *John*, 122.

[34] Carson, *Gospel According to John*, 246.

More than likely, it was a sin committed as a child. Following the logic of their argument, God disciplined this man through disability for a sin he committed as a child or young boy.

Köstenberger disagrees with Whitacre and Carson. He states that the implication of Jesus's statement is directed to eternal judgment for sin rather than a particular sin in this man's life.[35] Morris acknowledges the potential connection between sin and a worse physical fate. However, he sides with interpreting this statement of Jesus as underscoring the eternal consequences of sin. These consequences are far worse than any physical handicap.[36] Accordingly, George R. Beasley-Murray attributes this as a warning to the man that he may end up in Gehenna, if he continues his sinful ways.[37] Thus, these three scholars focus on the reality of sin or the lack of faith in this man's life, and what that will mean for his eternal destination. His failure to acknowledge Jesus as the Messiah puts him in jeopardy of forfeiting his very soul.

Kok wisely analyzes what is taking place in this temple meeting between Jesus and the man he has healed:

> In ordering the man not to sin anymore, Jesus communicates to him, firstly, that he has been touched, secondly, that he must realize who it was that made him whole, and thirdly, that he must start living within that relationship. However, by not knowing who Jesus really is, the man brings judgment upon himself. He is an unbeliever who fails to realize the true identity of Jesus.[38]

In this story, the lame man exhibits a clear lack of faith. This absence of faith is not simply a one-time experience for this man. On two occasions, he had the opportunity to acknowledge something about the one who has

---

[35] Köstenberger, *John*, 182.

[36] Morris, *Luke*, 172 (see chap. 6, n. 8).

[37] George R. Beasley-Murray, *John*, Word Biblical Commentary (Nashville: Thomas Nelson, 1999), 74.

[38] Kok, *New Perspectives on Healing, Restoration, and Reconciliation in John's Gospel*, 129.

healed him. Yet this healing did not lead to a demonstration of faith. In fact, it led to the man reporting Jesus to his enemies.

For the church, implications drawn from this lack of faith pose a challenge for all ministry generally and disability ministry specifically: continuing to show mercy and love even when there is no profession of faith. In this healing miracle Jesus continued to display mercy and love even though faith was not professed.

In a church climate that often seems in a hurry to rush from evangelism to discipleship, this story asks the question, "Is the demonstration of divine love and mercy contingent on a declaration of faith?" To put it programmatically, "Is it acceptable if the food bank ministry has not brought anyone to Jesus Christ in the past year but has diligently replicated his love and mercy to the poor?" Make no mistake about it, the church is not simply a social organization designed to only meet physical needs. She has a mission to evangelize, baptize, and disciple. However, under this mission lies the method of imitating Christ's divine love and mercy even in the face of one who does not profess faith.

The lame man's lack of faith provides one additional implication for the church to heed. Sadly, issues of health and healing are often connected to faith. This premise understands a sufficient amount of faith will produce the desired healing. Yet, this story speaks against that notion. The lame man exhibited no faith in Jesus. He only offered excuses. One might argue that he was healed even though he did not believe he could be healed. His circumstances were greater than his faith. Nevertheless, Jesus was not hindered in his ability to heal him. This implication ought to provide caution to the church leader or church member who questions the faith of an ill or disabled person. Behind this question lies the incorrect theological assumption that God is impaired by the individual's faithless heart and mind. As we see in the story of the lame man, even no faith is not a deterrent to God's ability to heal.

(10)

Restoring the Sight of a Man Born Blind

(John 9:1–41)

One day as Jesus and his disciples were walking along the road, Jesus spotted a man born blind. When the disciples saw him as well, they asked Jesus to explain why the man was blind. Was it because of his sin or was it because of his parents' sin? Jesus responded by telling them the man's blindness was not because of personal or parental sin. Instead, his blindness presented the opportunity for the glory of God to be displayed. Having said this, Jesus spat on the ground and made mud. He scooped it up, placed it on the man's eyes, and then told him to go wash in the pool of Siloam. The man did as Jesus said and came back seeing.

This healing set off a series of confrontations. The man's neighbors recognized him but did not understand how he had regained his sight. The Pharisees asked the once-blind man's parents to explain how their son could now see. They did not want to answer, because they feared these religious leaders. As the religious leaders questioned the once-blind man, they became more and more frustrated with him and his connection to Jesus. Eventually, they decided to banish him from the synagogue.

Jesus heard that the man had been thrown out of the synagogue and went to meet him. When he found him, Jesus pressed the issue of faith with him. The man believed and followed Jesus. The Pharisees then began to question Jesus. In turn, Jesus told them a parable about shepherds and sheep. In the first part of this parable, he talked about the shepherd, and how the sheep only listen to the voice of the shepherd instead of robbers and thieves. The religious leaders did not understand what Jesus was trying to say in this parable. Jesus followed it up by switching the illustration and directly personalizing it. He said that he was the gate to and for the sheep. The only way to these sheep was through him. Jesus then switched back to the shepherd motif, and instead of talking about a shepherd, he called himself the good shepherd. He elaborated on what this meant for the care and concern he had for his sheep. Finally, he said that he would give his life to save his sheep and God would raise him back to life. At this, the Pharisees began to discuss if Jesus was demon possessed. They could not understand Jesus's actions, his claims, or his teachings.

Common Studies of Disability and John 9

A quick review of most biblical literature on disability or disability ministry will almost inevitably include space dedicated to the healing of the blind man in John 9. It would seem that the disciples' theological question about the connection of sin and disability is one of the catalysts for the scrutiny this chapter receives. A second possible reason for its continued use in biblical discussions on disability is related to the way a disabled man goes from faithless to a follower of Christ. Thus, it makes for an easy methodology of evangelism and discipleship regarding the disabled. This approach would be a profitable exploration, but it is not in keeping with the direction of this book. A third apparent reason for the inclusion of the healing in John 9 in most biblical discussions on disability is the contrast it presents to the healing in John 5. In John 9, the man born blind responds positively to the healing and becomes a follower of Jesus. The healing story in John 5 presents the opposite situation. Once the sick man is healed, he becomes an informant for the religious leaders rather than a follower of Jesus. Thus, much has already been written on how John 9 serves as a contrast to John 5 and will not be considered in this section.

Connecting John 9 and John 10: Another Way of Investigating the Healing of the Blind Man in John 9

One area is often neglected in disability-related studies of John 9. This area is the intended connection between John 9 and John 10. Following the healing of the blind man, Jesus moves to discuss his role as the good shepherd and how it is contrasted with the role occupied by the religious leaders. Their actions against the once-blind man spur this comparison. This connection has grand implications for the disability-inclusive pastor or church leader. For Jesus, leaders who lack the divine compassion and sympathy for the blind man give evidence that they are not true shepherds. Further, the inability of these leaders to recognize this divine compassion and mercy in Jesus also adds to their indictment.

Philip Wesley Comfort and Wendell C. Hawley state that John 10:1–21 is a carryover of Christ's comments to the Pharisees. The heart of these words centers on the way these religious leaders had treated the once-blind man. They had banished him from Judaism in general and the temple in particular. Thus, Jesus portrayed this man as anyone who leaves Judaism to follow Jesus. They are sheep following their shepherd.[1] Burge also takes this position. He argues that John 10:1–21 is a continuation of John 9, since no new audience is assumed, and John 10:21 refers to the blind man's healing. He summarizes that these opening verses demonstrate that the

---

[1] Philip Wesley Comfort and Wendell C. Hawley, *Opening John's Gospel and Epistles* (Carol Stream, IL: Tyndale, 2009), 137.

once-blind man did not follow the Pharisees because he did not recognize their voices. Like a sheep, this man knew the voice of the true shepherd, and he followed him rather than the false shepherds or Pharisees. Burge notes that John 10:1–21 serves to severely critique the failed leadership of the Pharisees in John 9.[2]

For Morris, the connection between John 9 and John 10 is evident in the opening words of John 10:1: "I assure you" (HCSB) or "Truly, Truly, I say to you" (ESV). Morris stresses that this phrase is not used elsewhere to begin a discourse. Rather, it is a technique used to follow up a previous teaching and serves as a connector between the forthcoming explanation and the prior instruction.[3]

Köstenberger summarizes the situation in a way that ought to bring about a foreboding sense to the discerning reader. He writes:

> Chapter 10 follows chapter 9 without transition (see also 10:21); thus, Jesus's audiences are likely the same. Jesus's healing of the blind man had led to the man's expulsion from the local synagogue, an act viewed by Jesus as an arrogant assertion of usurped authority that called for further comment. For the Pharisees were not only blind themselves (9:40–41); they were also "blind guides" (cf. Matt. 23:16, 24) who led astray those entrusted to their care. The dark backdrop of Jesus's good shepherd discourse is therefore the blatant irresponsibility of the Jewish religious leaders.[4]

Ben Rhodes notes the sensory connection that links John 10 to John 9. He indicates that Jesus switched from visual to aural imagery to explain to the Pharisees that the voice of the true shepherd is one that the sheep hear and follow. Further, Rhodes believes the sheep Jesus had in mind are both those in the present context, as well as all subsequent listeners. Thus, like the blind man, those who follow Jesus today have

---

[2] Burge, *John*, 286 (see chap. 9, n. 7).

[3] Morris, *Gospel According to John*, 446 (see chap. 9, n. 24).

[4] Köstenberger, *John*, 298 (see chap. 9. n. 3).

not seen him but have heard and responded to his voice as it is heard throughout the Scriptures.[5]

This connection between John 9 and John 10 is frequently missed in disability studies. The narrowed focus for disability research in John 9 concentrates on the blind man and his healing. This limitation causes the majority of material to be concentrated on the question of sin, the contrast with John 5, or an assumed pattern of discipleship. Studies that stop at the end of John 9 rather than continuing through into John 10 inevitably pay little attention to the discourse of Jesus throughout these two chapters. When these two chapters are viewed Christocentrically rather than anthropocentrically, it allows for two important questions that relate to this study. First, is the glory of God only revealed through healing? Second, how does the illuminating work of Jesus reveal who is the true shepherd and who is a false shepherd?

Is the Glory of God Only Revealed through Healing?

The typical interpretation of the healing of the man born blind often creates an awkward situation for those with a disability. Jesus's answer of "This came about so that God's works might be displayed in him" (John 9:3 CSB) and then the blind man's subsequent healing can leave those with a disability feeling as if their continued handicap is an affront to God.

John Piper's understanding of this passage affords the typical interpretation of the disciple's question of "who sinned" and Jesus's response about "God's works." Piper notes that Jesus moved the question from cause to purpose to affirm that this man's disability is for the display of God's work. In other words, "the explanation of the blindness lies not in the past causes but the future purposes."[6] Further, Piper contrasts this man's healing with

---

[5] Ben Rhodes, "Signs and Wonders: Disability in the Fourth Gospel," *Journal of the Christian Institute on Disability* 5, no. 1 (March 13, 2016): 65.

[6] John Piper and Tony Reinke, *Disability and the Sovereign Goodness of God* (Minneapolis: Desiring God, 2012), 11–16, https://www.desiringgod.org/books/disability-and-the-sovereign-goodness-of-god.

the lack of healing for Paul when he cries out to God for the removal of his thorn in the flesh. He argues that, in Paul's case, God's glory is revealed through sustaining Paul rather than delivering him. Therefore, "The blindness is for the glory of God. The thorn in the flesh is for the glory of God. The healing is for his glory, and the non-healing is for his glory."[7]

The effects of this understanding can take a toll on those who are disabled. This reality is especially true when they feel as if they are losing the battle of faith more than they are winning it. It is the emotional cry of those who sense that there is more personal effort than sustaining faith going into their daily survival. This viewpoint is genuinely communicated in "Open Letter from a Blind Disciple to a Sighted Savior" by John Hull:

> When we read about the blind man in John 9 the situation is different, but presents its own problems. Your disciples anticipated a connection between disability and sin with the question, "who did sin, this man or his parents, that he was born blind?" You rejected this suggestion, adding, "that God's works might be revealed in him" (v. 3). In other words, the man had been blind from birth not because of some parental sin but in order to create a sort of photo opportunity for you, Lord. When you spoke of God's works being revealed in the blind man, you were not referring to his blindness but to the restoration of his sight. The implication is that God's work cannot be seen in a blind person but only in a blind person becoming sighted.[8]

One can almost hear the anguish of Hull as he comes to terms with his own blindness and the common interpretation of this passage. Later, in the same piece, Hull will ask his Savior why he had no blind disciples. Instead,

---

[7] Piper and Reinke, 16.

[8] John Hull, "Open Letter from a Blind Disciple to a Sighted Savior," in *Borders, Boundaries, and the Bible*, ed. M. O'Kane (New York: Sheffield Academic, 2002), 161–62.

choosing to heal both the blind man in John 9 and Bartimaeus, so that their blindness was not part of their followership.

Both Hull and Piper have a narrow understanding of this passage. Their view is truncated by examining only John 9:3 rather than Jesus's full statement in John 9:3–5. Further curtailing their interpretation is their failure to connect the actions and conversations of John 9 to the teaching of Jesus in John 10. When these contextual adjustments are made, the implications of Jesus's initial statement in John 9:3 opens up. Within the immediate context (John 9:4–5), Jesus made three statements that brought clarity to the disciples' question and Jesus's response (John 9:1–3). First, Jesus said, "We must do the works of Him who sent Me while it is day" (John 9:4a). He followed that up by noting, "Night is coming when no one can work" (John 9:4b). Jesus concluded by stating, "As long as I am in the world, I am the light of the world" (John 9:5). These three statements asked the disciples to consider the time, who Jesus is, and the work they should be about.

Rhodes explains the connection between each of these three statements:

This sign story is about spiritual and physical blindness. Before the discovery of electricity, work took place during the day, when the light of the sun made it possible to see (lamps were expensive, small, and did not cast enough light for farming). In the presence of Jesus, the dark world is spiritually illuminated. That is why the religious authorities are without excuse: of all people, they should have been able to see, to understand his divine identity as revealed in the light of his signs. . . . Jesus is either saying that he is revealing the purposes of God in this man's life by his whole interaction with him (not merely by curing him) or that we (the disciples and the subsequent Christian community, including us as readers) are called to reveal God's purposes within disability by the way we respond to such individuals.[9]

---

[9] Rhodes, "Signs and Wonders," 67.

This attention to the glory of God on display is also the conclusion that Burge makes in his understanding of John 9:3–5. Burge insists that "Jesus must work so that God's work may be displayed in this man's life." As such, the man's blindness is not simply a purposed occasion for God to showcase his glory. Instead, Jesus's healing work in and of itself represents the work of God that puts God's glory on display.[10]

Carson further distances the man's blindness and curing as the singular evidence of God's glory. He argues that what is taking place in this episode is more than a miracle. This healing event is a sign that this Jesus is the long-awaited Messiah. Thus, these works of God, through Jesus, shed light into darkness and reveal the Messiah.[11] In this description, Carson echoes C. H. Dodd who explains that, for John, the signs are not simply miraculous acts. Instead, they are significant acts that represent a spiritual reality. Those who intuitively see and properly understand these signs grasp this spiritual reality.[12]

Köstenberger simplifies this understanding by expressing that the signs in John's Gospel point to the glory of God on display in Jesus. As such, these signs identify Jesus as God's true representative.[13]

When a concerted focus is only directed to John 9:3 instead of John 9:3–5, the result is attention only on the disciples' question and Jesus's answer. This misplaced prominence puts an emphasis on the blind man's healing as it relates to the work or glory of God. This error creates the tension experienced by those who are disabled as they wonder if the primary way God receives glory through their disability would be through healing. However, when the full response of Jesus is considered, the focus shifts from the blind man's healing to the revelation and work of Jesus Christ. In this significant healing sign, God was glorified through

---

[10] Burge, *John*, 273 (see chap. 9, n. 7).

[11] Carson, *Gospel According to John*, 363 (see chap. 9. n. 5).

[12] C. H. Dodd, *The Interpretation of the Fourth Gospel* (Cambridge: Cambridge University, 1953), 90.

[13] Andreas J. Köstenberger, *A Theology of John's Gospel and Letters*, Biblical Theology of the New Testament (Grand Rapids: Zondervan, 2009), 327.

the visual validation that Jesus Christ is the Messiah and his representative. Thus, the focus is shifted from the blind man and directed to both God the Father and God the Son.

Further, the initial contextual understanding of this healing episode becomes even more direct when it is combined with the relative direction of this healing story. Jesus's work, as the true shepherd, is to call out to those who would hear his voice, recognize it, and then follow him. For this once-blind man, he was being called out of Judaism and into a life of following the true shepherd. Further, this work would also become the task of the disciples. They too would call people out of their religious and philosophical structures and into a life of discipleship represented by following Jesus. As Jesus models in John 9, this call to follow him is not conditioned on social status or religious performance. Certainly, the once-blind man would not have either of these two qualifications. However, he heard and followed the call of the true shepherd.

How Does the Illuminating Work of Jesus Reveal Who Is the True Shepherd and Who Is a False Shepherd?: Of Metaphors and Models

The ongoing dialogue between Jesus, the once-blind man, and the religious leaders led to the man becoming a follower of Jesus and to his expulsion from the synagogue. As a result of this dismissal, Jesus addressed the way the Pharisees had reacted to him, the once-blind man's healing, and his ensuing declaration about Jesus (John 10:1–19). Using a common cultural image combined with the prophetic words of Ezekiel, Jesus identified himself as the good shepherd while the religious leaders were more like the evil shepherds spoken of in Ezekiel 34. This profound illustration tells us much about the work of God that Jesus knew he and his disciples needed to accomplish. However, Jesus also mixed the metaphor in this section. He called himself the door, or the gate, to the sheep pen. This metaphor allowed him to juxtapose his character with those he considers thieves and robbers. Both the image of the good shepherd and the door to the sheep pen are images worth exploring because of the implications each of these have for disability ministry.

To understand an image that can easily be lost in a non-agrarian culture, a short summary of the life of a shepherd is necessary. R. C. Sproul succinctly outlines the daily routine of a shepherd:

> In those days, there was one large, central pen, or sheepfold, in a given community, and at the end of the day people brought their small individual flocks and led them into the big sheepfold. With their combined resources, they paid a gatekeeper, and it was his job to stay with the sheep during the night. In the morning, the gatekeeper opened the gate to those who were truly shepherds, whose sheep were enclosed in the sheepfold. The shepherds entered by the door, for they had every right to do so—the sheep were theirs and the gatekeeper was their paid servant. When a shepherd entered the sheepfold, the sheep of all the local flocks were mixed, but he began to call, and his sheep recognized his voice and came to him. In fact, a good shepherd was so intimately involved with the care and the nurture of his sheep that he had names for them, and he would call them by name. His sheep followed him out because they knew him.[14]

This description sheds light on the metaphor Jesus used. As the shepherd, he enters the sheep fold appropriately, he knows his sheep, he calls his sheep, he leads them out, and they follow him because they know his voice. Each of these elements is represented in the work God has sent Jesus to do (John 9:4–5). This job description of a shepherd also served as a point of condemnation for the Pharisees. Jesus identified them as the false shepherds.

In Jesus's illustration, the bond described between the shepherd and his sheep draws attention to four relational qualities that exist between

---

[14] R. C. Sproul, *John*, St. Andrew's Expositional Commentary (Lake Mary, FL: Reformation Trust, 2009), 187.

the master and his flock. The first section of John 10:1–21 points to the relational qualities of intimacy and trust (vv. 1–6). The second section of John 10:1–21 addresses the relational quality of accessibility (vv. 7–10). Finally, the third section of John 10:1–21 speaks to the relational quality of sacrifice (vv. 11–21).

Intimacy and Trust (John 10:1–6)

Kenneth O. Gangel suggests that the active verbs of opens, listen, calls, and leads, of John 10:3 (NIV) are important to understanding the relationship between the shepherd and his sheep. Specifically, he believes these four words are indicative of the affection that exists between them. Supporting this claim, Gangel emphasizes that the shepherd calls his sheep by name. His call is not simply a singular address to the whole flock. Further, Gangel notes that John also uses the phrase "by name" in his third epistle where he tells Gaius, "The friends send you greetings. Greet the friends by name" (3 John 14).[15] Contextually then, there is a friendly and affectionate connotation to the way the shepherd calls his own sheep. He is not simply addressing them as a group. Instead, knowing each of his sheep individually, he calls them by name. Charles Thomas Wilson further develops this imagery pointing to John 10:3 and revealing that, "The shepherds often give names to their sheep. These names are descriptive of some trait or characteristic of the animal, as Long-ears, White-nose, Speckled, and so forth. Not unfrequently the sheep get to know their names and will answer to them when called."[16]

More recently, Craig S. Keener also demonstrates that shepherds individually named and called their sheep by those names. He notes that shepherds preferred a shorter name like "snowy" since this allowed for quickly calling the animals. Additionally, names were often selected based

---

[15] Kenneth O. Gangel, *John* (Nashville: B&H, 2000), 195–96.

[16] Charles Thomas Wilson, *Peasant Life in the Holy Land* (London: J. Murray, 1906), 165.

on shape, color, or peculiarities. This naming practice is indicative of familiarity and affection.[17]

There may be some danger in blurring the illustrative lines between this shepherding practice and the present-day domestication of cats and dogs. Perhaps it may be helpful though, since most modern North American Christians have little familiarity with shepherding. When one brings home a cat or a dog, one of the first tasks is to select a suitable name. The naming of the animal only increases the level of affection between the owner and that cat or dog. This is the type of affection Jesus was trying to impress upon the religious leaders and all who were overhearing this discussion with this shepherd and sheep imagery. There is an intimacy between the shepherd and his sheep. This human/animal affection is akin to the type of affection the modern human beings have for their pets. Köstenberger nicely summarizes the meaning of Jesus's metaphor when he writes, "This intimacy of shepherd and his flock provides a beautiful illustration of the trust, familiarity, and bond existing between Jesus and his followers."[18]

In the previous quotation, Köstenberger mentions a second important relational quality—trust. Herman N. Ridderbos recognizes a level of trust that exists between the shepherd and the sheep. When the sheep hear his voice, their ears prick up. They become attentive as he calls them by their familiar names. They follow him as he leads them out. For the shepherd, he only moves on once he is sure every one of his sheep have left the fold. Then, and only then, does he place himself in front of them as he leads them to pasture. The shepherd is familiar to the sheep and the sheep are familiar to the shepherd.[19]

It is this connection to the voice of the shepherd that shows the trust the sheep have in the shepherd. Carson suggests it is simply because the

---

[17] Craig S. Keener, *The Gospel of John: A Commentary* (Peabody, MA: Hendrickson, 2003), 805.

[18] Köstenberger, *John*, 302 (see chap. 9, n. 3).

[19] Herman N. Ridderbos, *The Gospel According to John: A Theological Commentary* (Grand Rapids: Eerdmans, 1997), 355.

sheep know the shepherd's voice that they follow him. Their following from familiarity stands against their inattentiveness to the voice of a stranger. They do not follow the stranger, because they do not recognize his voice.[20] Ernst Haenchen also demonstrates this understanding: "That the sheep follow him because they recognize his voice shows that they trust him."[21] Thus, the trust connection between the sheep and the shepherd is related to their familiarity to his voice. The shepherd recognizes each one of them as his own. However, the inverse is also true. The sheep are so in tune with the voice of the shepherd they obediently come and follow when they hear his voice. When another voice appeals for them to follow him as their shepherd, the sheep do not recognize the voice and will not trust that shepherd.

Interestingly, Tenney moves the issue of trust beyond the aural to the experiential. He notes that the shepherd has the right to enter the fold at any time and that he commands the attention of the sheep. Additionally, the sheep follow him because they trust his leadership. Tenney makes this assumption as a means of connecting the shepherd of John 10:1–6 to the good shepherd of John 10:11–21.[22] While this makes sense in terms of Jesus as the good shepherd, it would be difficult to evaluate how much a sheep can comprehend of a shepherd's leadership. It seems more probable to leave the connection of trust to the reality of vocal familiarity.

The shepherd's knowledge of and affection for the sheep establish a meaningful relationship between them. This relationship creates an environment where the sheep can discern and hear the voice of their shepherd. Consequently, they follow the shepherd as he leads them out of the sheep pen and into pasture. Underscoring the action of the sheep is the trust they have placed in their shepherd. He is one who knows their name, calls them by that name, and faithfully leads them.

---

[20] Carson, *Gospel According to John*, 383.

[21] Ernst Haenchen, *John: A Commentary on the Gospel of John*, vol. 2, Hermeneia (Philadelphia: Fortress, 1984), 2:47.

[22] Tenney, *John*, 163–65 (see chap. 9, n. 12).

Kenneth E. Bailey makes a poignant and practical observation. He draws application from a sheep's ability to hear, identify, and follow the shepherd's voice. Even though Jesus's illustration is rooted in an agrarian culture, Bailey sees it as having utmost relevance for today's technologically driven culture:

> In passing we can observe that this text is extraordinarily contemporary. With the information technology that surrounds us, never in human history have there been as many divergent, strident voices calling loudly for the attention and loyalty of "the flock." Daily the sheep must consciously seek to ignore those noises and listen for the voice of their good shepherd and follow it.[23]

Considering the issue of trust that has been explored here, it stands to reason that Christ-followers today reveal the level of trust they have in their good shepherd by their willingness to block out the other voices that clamor for their attention. Just as the sheep in Jesus's illustration only follow the voice of the shepherd and flee from the voice of the stranger, so believers must do the same. The still small voice of Jesus must become so familiar to them that it is easily heard among a crescendo of cultural voices.

Accessibility (John 10:7–10)

The third relational quality is that of accessibility. In John 10:7–10, Jesus changed the metaphor so that he was then the door or the gate to the sheep pen. In making this switch Jesus was highlighting his dual role. He is the one who has sole access to the sheep, as well as the only way the sheep can experience salvation and blessing.

These two functions are crucial to Ridderbos's understanding of John 10:7–10. Ridderbos understands Jesus's use of the door or gate to be indicative of his accessibility to the sheep. Only Jesus, as the gate, has the ability to get to the sheep. Thus, the shepherd serves to protect and keep his sheep

---

[23] Kenneth E. Bailey, *The Good Shepherd: A Thousand-Year Journey From Psalm 23 to the New Testament* (Downers Grove, IL: InterVarsity, 2014), 219.

safe. However, Ridderbos also acknowledges that Jesus is also the gate that leads to salvation for the sheep. In other words, the salvation, safety, and security of the sheep only happen if they go through the gate.[24] Hendriksen identifies a similar thought by pointing out that Jesus is both the door to the sheep and the door for the sheep. Thus, the dual nature of this illustration is appropriate because it highlights the in-and-out function of a door.[25]

However, consideration must be given to the fact that Jesus's extension or alteration of his metaphor rests on the fact that those listening to him did not understand it when it was first presented (John 10:6). Thus, it would be unwise to miss possible connections to the opening metaphor in John 10:1–6. These connections are something that Burge addresses in his understanding of John 10:7–10. Burge depicts the full image of this shepherd/gate metaphor when he points to both the security and the prosperity of the sheep. The picture being developed is one of vulnerable sheep that are protected from the predators that surround them. They cannot enter the sheep pen. However, the sheep are also well-fed since they are daily led to water and pastures. The sheep described in this metaphor are ones that are content and flourishing because of the skill of the shepherd.[26] Timothy S. Laniak agrees with Burge and supports this emphasis when both metaphors are understood together:

> [Jesus] identifies himself as both door and shepherd. As the door, he is the exclusive means of entrance into the protected fold. As the shepherd, he is the one who leads the flock to pastures (abundant life). By both metaphors, Jesus contrasts himself with others—those who do not use the door and those who care for themselves rather than the flock.[27]

---

[24] Ridderbos, *Gospel According to John*, 358.

[25] Hendriksen, *Exposition of the Gospel According to John*, 1:108 (see chap. 9, n. 20).

[26] Burge, *John*, 290.

[27] Timothy S. Laniak, *Shepherds After My Own Heart: Pastoral Traditions and Leadership in the Bible*, New Studies in Biblical Theology 20 (Downers Grove, IL: InterVarsity, 2006), 214.

Burge and Laniak are not the only commentators to recognize the benefits Jesus provides in this continued metaphor. Much earlier, B. F. Westcott
also made a similar connection to the robust nature of Jesus's two metaphors. However, Westcott sees three benefits provided by Jesus instead of
just the two given by Burge. Westcott sees in Jesus's pronouncement of "I
am the door. If anyone enters by Me, he will be saved and will come in and
go out and find pasture" (John 10:9) as Jesus's provision of the three elements in a full Christian life. These elements are safety, liberty, and support.
Thus, Jesus as the gate is the one who can bring protection to his sheep. This
sense of protection leads his sheep to living in a freedom that is represented
by the in-and-out nature of their activities. Finally, it is because of Jesus that
his sheep find the sustenance they need in their daily lives.[28]

What makes Jesus's door/gate pronouncement crucial for disability concerns is that this teaching follows the healing of a man born blind. In this
healing, Jesus has just granted accessibility to a man who had never had any
of it because of his disability. Bruce J. Malina and Richard L. Rohrbaugh
explain that in this time and culture the primary problem with sickness was
the removing of the sick person from both their social mooring and social
standing. Socialization between family members, friends, neighbors, and
village mates was stopped. When healing occurred, then restoration to the
social network would be permitted.[29]

Given this information, the once-blind man was shut out of any social
network for his entire life. Additionally, he was known by his neighbors as
a beggar (John 9:8). This way of life would have further devalued his social
standing. The fact that John records the Pharisees having conversations with
the neighbors and parents of the once-blind man is indicative of the fact
that his life was not completely alone. This factor is one of the differences
between the lame man in John 5 and the blind man in John 9. However,

---

[28] B. F. Westcott, *The Gospel According to St. John* (Grand Rapids: Eerdmans,
1978), 153.

[29] Bruce J. Malina and Richard L. Rohrbaugh, *Social-Science Commentary on
the Gospel of John* (Minneapolis: Fortress, 1998), 113–14.

these relationships could not have been deeply meaningful. Both the man's neighbors and his parents quickly recused themselves when pressed about the healing. Thus, Jesus's healing of the man provided him with accessibility to a social network within the followers of Jesus as well as eternal accessibility to heaven.

This model of accessibility is an important consideration for the church as it thinks through purposeful disability ministry. Accessibility should be spiritual, physical, and social. Spiritual accessibility takes into consideration a purposeful outreach to the disabled community so that they have the opportunity to hear the gospel in a way that is understandable. Spiritual accessibility also gives thought to what the process of discipleship should like for those who are disabled and, in their own way, made a profession of faith in Jesus Christ. Spiritual accessibility also seeks to give those who have a disability the opportunity to use and share their spiritual gifts with the community of faith.

Physical accessibility means that a congregation has measured the ways a disabled person might face challenges due to the church building as they participate in the full body life of the church. Issues such as handicapped parking or handicapped seating as well as access to restrooms are significant places to begin.

Social accessibility revolves around establishing a network that will support, encourage, and involve those who are disabled in the various programs of the church. Additionally, it goes one step further and seeks to find ways to connect those who are disabled to other members of the church in ways that are not programmatically driven.

Only when each of these accessibility points are met will the church reverse the conclusion made by Nancy L. Eiesland when she wrote, "For many disabled persons the church has been a 'city on a hill'—physically inaccessible and socially inhospitable."[30]

---

[30] Nancy L. Eiesland, *The Disabled God: Toward a Liberatory Theology of Disability* (Nashville: Abingdon, 1994), 20.

Sacrifice (John 10:11–21)

Jesus moved from describing the shepherd in John 10:1–15 to describing the good shepherd in John 10:11–18. In this progression, he identified himself as the good shepherd. The overuse of the word *good* in our culture can contribute to a misunderstanding of how the *good* in "good shepherd" should be defined. Laniak gives two reasons that *kalos*, the word used for *good*, should be translated as *model* instead of *good*. First, a common understanding of *good* often relates to nothing more than a moral quality. However, the term *kalos* implies more than this. Laniak writes, "*Kalos* implies an attractive quality, something noble or ideal."[31] Thus, a term like *model* better captures this imagery. Secondly, *kalos* implies emulation. As such, *model* also underscores this much more accurately than *good*. This emphasis on Jesus as the *model* shepherd also fits with John's perspective that Jesus was equipping the disciples to be like him in both his life and his death.[32]

Grammatically, it is best to understand that Jesus's movement from a shepherd to the good shepherd was about the type of shepherd one should use as a model. Yet this is not simply a point of grammar. Jesus was pointing out that he alone is the good shepherd and that those who follow him should model his sense of shepherding. Jesus was not simply suggesting that one be a good shepherd by selecting a model that is comfortable for them. The designation of a good shepherd is not attributed to a subjective image. Instead, the good shepherd or model shepherd is Jesus Christ. One who is committed to Christ and follows his life acknowledges that they have a particular model in mind.

To demonstrate what makes up a model shepherd, Jesus contrasted himself to a hireling. Primarily he noted that the hireling does not care about the sheep and will run at the first sign of life-threatening trouble (John 10:12–13). The hired man places a greater value on his life than that of his sheep. Laniak recognizes that, in making this contrast, Jesus was pushing the

---

[31] Laniak, *Shepherds After My Own Heart*, 211.
[32] Laniak, 211.

boundaries of the metaphor. Shepherds would occasionally risk their life for their sheep. However, it would be unheard of for a shepherd to deliberately die for the protection and safety of the sheep he loves. Laniak perceptively summarizes, "Life for the predator entails death for the flock; life for the flock requires death for the shepherd."[33]

In an escalating fashion, Keener describes the model shepherd as one who cared for his sick sheep, so that they were restored to health. The faithful and model shepherd's life was difficult and would require that he face predators to protect the sheep. Sometimes, facing a predator, robber, or thief may cost the faithful shepherd his life. However, a faithful shepherd who loved his sheep and would give us his own life for these sheep would astound listeners.[34]

Both Laniak and Keener highlight the shock value of Jesus's further development of his metaphorical teaching on the blind man's healing. Jesus, as the model shepherd, does something no shepherd in their right mind would consider doing. Yet, the model shepherd freely gives up his life for his own sheep. At the center of the model shepherd's self-sacrifice is a heart of love. The hired man runs when wolves, thieves, or robbers arrive. His self-preservation and commitment to the monetary gains of shepherding will not allow him to fight for the sheep, much less give his life for the sheep. The same cannot be said about the model shepherd.

John Quasten highlights two reasons why the model shepherd will lay down his life for his sheep. First, the good shepherd cares for his sheep (John 10:11–13). Second, the good shepherd knows his sheep (John 10:14–15). These two reasons establish the primary character quality of the good shepherd. He is the one who is not afraid to give up his life for the sake of his sheep. Further, this self-sacrifice is indicative of the freedom of will possessed by the good shepherd.[35]

---

[33] Laniak, 216.

[34] Keener, *Gospel of John*, 813–14.

[35] John Quasten, "The Parable of the Good Shepherd: JN. 10:1–21 (Continued)," *Catholic Biblical Quarterly* 10, no. 2 (1948): 161.

What does it look like for the model shepherd to care for his sheep? In other words, why would the model shepherd stay and die for his sheep rather than flee like a hired man does when trouble comes? Morris provides the answer as he explains the reasons for the actions of the hired man:

> The hired hand runs away not fortuitously, but because he is what he is, hired. His interest is in wages not sheep. He is not deeply concerned for the sheep. He is not involved in their situation. His passions are not aroused. The interests of the sheep are not a lively concern for him.[36]

The model shepherd, on the other hand, is concerned for his sheep. He is passionately involved in their situation so that their existence is one of protection and provision (John 10:9). This is heightened by the fact that the model shepherd knows them. In fact, he calls them by name (John 10:3). Further, according to Jesus, that knowledge is similar to the way he knows his Father God, and the way God the Father knows him. Burge explains this and the important application of the model shepherd's knowledge:

> Perhaps the most startling feature of Jesus' interpretation is his description of the intimacy of the sheep and the shepherd. We have already learned that the sheep "know" the shepherd's voice (10:4), but now we learn that this knowledge is mutual and exhaustive (10:14). Moreover, the model for this intimacy is the mutual knowledge shared between the Son and the Father—and here Jesus slips out of the parable and speaks directly of himself and God (cf. Matt. 11:27). His profound relationship with God characterizes the intimacy he seeks with his followers (17:21); as he and the Father share profound love, so too Jesus and his flock share this quality of love.[37]

---

[36] Morris, *Gospel According to John*, 455 (see chap. 9, n. 24).

[37] Burge, *John*, 291.

Burge ties together both the caring or love of the model shepherd in John 10:11–13 and the knowledge of the good shepherd in John 10:14–15. In doing so, Burge is able to argue that the model for this mutual and exhaustive relationship is the reciprocal relational knowledge between Jesus and God.[38] Quasten also ties together this knowledge and love. He claims that the knowledge identified in John 10:14 is not a theoretical knowledge of "the Father's splendor, power, love, and fidelity." Rather, this knowledge represents "the most profound communion of love." This love is rooted in the attentive and considerate affection of the shepherd. This reciprocal knowledge, underscored by love, creates the readiness for the self-sacrifice of the shepherd.[39] The intimacy shared between God the Father and God the Son is the model for the intimacy of the shepherd and the sheep. It is a model that highlights a knowledge that goes beyond just knowing about someone. It's a loving knowledge of that person. Indeed, for the shepherd, it's a loving knowledge that will lead to his willingness to lay down his life for his sheep. This sacrifice is the ultimate blessing of eternal protection and provision.

The Good Shepherd Model of the Church

Taken as a whole, the four relational qualities just discussed create the type of communal environment that allows those with disabilities to thrive. An accessible community where trust, intimacy, and sacrifice are leading hallmarks makes for an approachable and welcoming church. It is a community where accessibility goes beyond just a blue sticker acknowledging the intentional structure of the building. It is the type of community that recognizes that an accessible church is reflected in both structure and attitudes.

These qualities also create a climate that will separate the community of faith from the cultural communities that surround it. While accessibility

---

[38] Burge, 291.

[39] Quasten, "The Parable of the Good Shepherd," 162.

is a government mandate for the alteration of buildings, it is ineffective in altering the attitudes found in the hearts of human beings. Consequently, the relational qualities of trust, intimacy, and sacrifice are difficult to find in most societal environments. However, God's people are called to a standard higher than the accessibility measures mandated by the government. If Christians truly embraced this standard, so that the church became a beacon pointing to an accessible community of trust, intimacy, and sacrifice, their witness to the disabled community would increase exponentially. Those who find themselves marginalized by disability would recognize within the community of faith a welcoming environment that traces the pattern created by the model shepherd.

11

Jesus, John's Gospel, and Inclusive Leadership

N ow that we have examined the two relevant passages from John 5 and 9–10, consideration can once again be given to Echols's five critical characteristics of inclusive leadership. Echols argues that inclusive leadership demonstrates the following five characteristics:

1. Maximum Participation: Inclusive leadership brings the maximum number of individuals into participation.

2. Individual Empowerment: Inclusive leadership empowers individuals to reach their full potential while pursuing the common good of the particular populace.

3. Worth of the Individual: Inclusive leadership develops a culture that perpetuates the morality of the worth of the individual in such a way as to act as a preventive resistance against the ever-present possibility of despotism.

4. Replication of Inclusive Leaders: Inclusive leadership is intentional in the replication of today's leaders who model the above

characteristics with a commitment to allow future leadership to emerge.

5.   Boundary Development: Inclusive leadership is manifested in the development of appropriate boundaries that maintain the integrity of the nature of the collective without marginalizing any of the populace.[1]

The question to be evaluated is, does the leadership example left by Jesus in John 5 and John 9–10 resemble the qualities proposed by Echols for an inclusive leader?

Jesus and Maximum Participation

In both stories an individual is targeted. In John 5, Jesus selected a man waiting to be healed around the pool of Bethesda. In John 9–10, Jesus saw a blind man and moved to heal him. While both healing stories circle around an individual, the ripples reached out to many others. It was not simply the lame man or the blind man who was impacted by their encounters with Jesus.

In John 5, the actions taken by the lame man brought him face-to-face with the religious authorities. He had to speak to his Sabbath rule-breaking. He could only muster an answer that amounts to, "He told me to." This heightened the sense of intrigue for both the religious leaders and the healed man. Why would a healer, if he was indeed from God, intentionally break the Sabbath? Later, when Jesus met him again in the temple complex area, Jesus revealed to the once-lame man who he was. In turn, the man informed the religious leaders that it was Jesus who healed him. Thus, they were once again brought into a participatory circle in this healing episode.

Jesus's question to the man as he lay around the pool waiting for the healing waters to be stirred can also be seen in a participatory manner. Jesus asked the man if he wanted to get well. This question was the opportunity for

---

[1] Echols, "Transformational/Servant Leadership," 88–91 (see chap. 1, n. 15).

this man to speak for himself and declare his intentions. However, instead of affirming his desire, the man simply provided a list of excuses for his inability to be healed. This emphasizes his belief that perhaps Jesus would stay with him and assist him when the waters stirred. Instead of dismissing his reasons, Jesus read the deep desire of the man's heart flooded over by these excuses. Jesus told him to pick up his mat and walk. Once again, the man was given an opportunity to participate in the healing through obedience. These two statements in Jesus's conversation with the lame man demonstrate a participatory bent in Jesus's encounters with the disabled.

Finally, when Jesus caught up with the man again, it was in the temple complex. This second encounter reflects how this healing was the opportunity for the man to leave a life of marginalization and reenter the religious life of his culture. He was given the opportunity to participate in both the religious and social networks of his day. He had moved from segregation to participation. Additionally, in this second encounter, Jesus pressed the issue of faith and belief. Here was a man who had accepted the healing of Jesus but was not participating in the salvation offered by Jesus. In response, Jesus confronted him with the reality of the eternal implications in only seeing Jesus as a healer, as opposed to Jesus as the Savior. Jesus's pursuit of the once-lame man is indicative of an inclusive leader who seeks maximum participation from a person who has a limited perspective of Jesus.

One possible argument against maximum participation in this story is that only one of the people gathered around the pool was healed. John 5 tells us that a large number of the blind, lame, and paralyzed gathered around the pool. Yet, rather than healing multiple people, or all of the people there, Jesus healed one man and then quietly slipped away (John 5:13). It would seem that more healings would result in maximum participation. At the risk of over-spiritualizing this story, there is a way in which from this one man, maximum participation was achieved. The character quality of this man was certainly suspicious. His portrayal in this narrative is more negative than positive. This negative portrayal includes offering complaints, lacking faith, and appearing ungrateful to be healed. Regardless of these issues, Jesus healed him anyway. In so doing, a picture of God's grace is revealed through this man. It is a picture of God's grace that is still relevant and powerful today. God's grace is effective to reach any condition. It will even heal an ungrateful complainer who cannot fathom how he could be healed. It is this kind of grace that calls to individuals today, seeking to engage them in participation of kingdom life.

John 9, which contains the healing of the blind man, is a little more straightforward when it comes to maximum participation. From the healing of this one man, neighbors, family members, Jesus's disciples, and the religious leaders were all brought into this miracle. The concentric circle spirals outward, encompassing more and more people as the story develops over two chapters.

The blind man's participation grew as he moved from seeing Jesus as merely a prophet from God to the Savior sent by God. As the man was challenged by the religious leaders or encouraged by Jesus, his level of kingdom participation increased. The neighbors and parents of the once-blind man were also drawn into the healing through the investigation of the religious leaders. They had the opportunity to participate in the healing and the kingdom by acknowledging their spiritual blindness. However, like the lame man in John 5, the parents and the neighbors declined the invitation because of the presence of the religious leaders. They acknowledged that something significant had happened to this once-blind man, but they refused to participate in the healing with any further acknowledgment.

The religious leaders were also invited to participate in this healing miracle by acknowledging the work God had accomplished through Jesus. However, their spiritual blindness remained as they refused to believe that Jesus was the Messiah. The good shepherd parable in John 10 is further testimony to Jesus's desire for maximum participation. Rather than simply walking out when the Pharisees refused to believe, Jesus elaborated on what had just transpired in the healing of the blind man. This teaching was designed to give these religious leaders one more opportunity to participate in the kingdom. However, their willful ignorance remained, and they refused to see Jesus as the long-awaited Messiah.

As an inclusive leader, Jesus sought maximum participation from those he encountered as he performed these healing miracles. John's account of two of these miracles demonstrates how Jesus was not content to let a healing miracle exist as an isolated event. Rather, they were opportunities for him to engage those within the proximity of the miracle. This encounter presented them with the prospect of recognizing Jesus as the Messiah and participating in the new kingdom.

Jesus and Individual Empowerment

As with the healing stories in the Synoptic Gospels, these two healings demonstrate Jesus's commitment to empowering an individual. This empowerment stands over and against a culture that had removed any power from these individuals on account of their disability. Both men were powerless when Jesus encountered them. Through Jesus's healing they regained physical power. The removal of a disability and the restoration of physical power placed each of these men back into the religious, familial, and social networks of their culture. They were empowered to participate in each of these networks in ways that were not possible while they were lame or blind. Perhaps the greatest evidence of this empowerment is found in the presence of the synagogue and religious leaders in each narrative. Both the once-lame and once-blind man had significant interactions with the religious leaders as it related to their role in adherence to religious legalities. These conversations, as well as their admittance into the synagogue, would have been impossible without the empowerment of Jesus through healing.

However, there was also an individual spiritual empowerment at work as well. This spiritual empowerment is characterized in John 1:12: "But to all who did receive Him, He gave them the right to be children of God, to those who believe in His name." After the healing, each man's additional encounter with Jesus was designed to engage them in a spiritual conversation that would move the healing from a physical reality to a spiritual one. It was designed to encourage them to receive Jesus as the Messiah and become children of God. This new relationship is a spiritual empowerment that enables individuals to become children of God.

For the once-lame man of John 5, this conversation centered on the real and eternal danger of remaining in sin. Only the recognition of Jesus as the Messiah, rather than simply as a healer, would prevent this eternal danger. This conversation amounted to the spiritual empowerment of the once-lame man. He had been empowered physically, but would he accept the spiritual empowerment offered by Jesus? Every indication from the text is that he rejected the full potential of his healing and spiritual empowerment by leaving Jesus and turning to the religious leaders.

The once-blind man in John 9 had a second encounter with Jesus that moved him from physical healing to spiritual healing. He recognized and received Jesus as the Messiah and, as such, became a child of God. This belief led to his expulsion from the synagogue. Ironically, the religious leaders viewed their imposed banishment as the removal of spiritual empowerment. No longer would this man be able to access God through the rites and rituals of Judaism. However, what the once-blind man had received was a spiritual empowerment that was much deeper and more profound than the religious leaders could have ever imagined. This man now had access directly to God through the person of Jesus Christ. He had become a child of God, with all of its rights and privileges. As a child of God, he was spiritually empowered to reach his full potential in ways that would never be possible through the legalistic framework of the enforced law of the Pharisees.

Jesus's encounter with a lame man and a blind man reveal that his healings were not simply about restoring something physical that had been lost. He was interested in more than just restoring the ability to walk or the ability to see. These abilities would empower individuals to achieve something physically that they were not capable of before they met Jesus; however, the healing miracles performed by Jesus were also a sign indicating that he was indeed the Messiah. As such, each of these healings were designed to move from physical empowerment to spiritual empowerment. They were designed to empower individuals with the right to become children of God. This empowerment was a spiritual empowerment that would have been lost to those who had a disability under the old framework of Pharisaic Judaism. Their exclusion from the various forms of temple and synagogue worship left them stigmatized and marginalized rather than empowered. As an inclusive leader, Jesus liberated these two individuals from the imposed religious obligations. However, their healing also presented each of them with an opportunity for a greater spiritual empowerment as children of God. It was only the once-blind man who recognized this.

Jesus and the Worth of the Individual

John 5 and John 9 are examples of how Jesus saw value in individuals who, according to their culture, had little value. Jerome H. Neyrey argues that during this period the classification of people could be mapped into ten categories. These categories can be ranked based on wholeness so that those most whole are those who are most holy. Thus, people were ranked as follows: priests, Levites, Israelites, converts, free slaves, disqualified priests, netzins (or, netizens, that is, temple slaves), mamzers (bastards), those with damaged testicles, and those without a penis. Neyrey notes that this list demonstrates a progression of worth based on wholeness. Thus, those who were physically damaged were last, and those whose family line was damaged are second to last. Conversely, the priests are first due to their ability to go into the holy of holies. They were followed by the Levites since they were permitted to enter the sanctuary. The third position was occupied by the Israelites due to their ability to stand in the courts. A sociocultural ranking system such as this allowed people to know exactly where they stood in the culture.[2]

---

[2] Jerome H. Neyrey, ed., *The Social World of Luke-Acts: Models for Interpretation* (Peabody, MA: Hendrickson, 1991), 279.

It was into this system that Jesus rewrote the idea of individual worth. He did not see individuals based on this standard of wholeness and holiness. Thus, the lame man in John 5 and the blind man in John 9 did not have a standing that relegated either of them to the end of a list. Had Jesus merely viewed them as categories on a list, they would have been marked as unclean and therefore unapproachable. Yet, Jesus went out of his way to meet with the lame man around the pool of Bethesda. He also purposefully talked to and touched the blind man to facilitate his healing.

The healing of the lame man in John 5 also shows that Jesus willingly chose to visit a place where many who were socioculturally unclean were placed. This locale represented the kind of area that the Pharisees and religious leaders would purposefully avoid. This abstention would have been even truer when a specific Jewish feast was approaching. To be at such a gathering of unclean individuals would most certainly lead to the transference of uncleanness. This would result in the inability to participate in that particular feast. However, for Jesus, what deserved more consideration was not the potential for exclusion from a feast but ministering to a lame and unclean man at the pool of Bethesda. Just as Jesus demonstrated the willingness to heal on a Sabbath day, he also demonstrated the willingness to heal around the feast days. The potential of contamination from uncleanliness took a backseat to Jesus's desire to restore the lame man's health. His value or worth, regardless of the sociocultural perception, took precedence.

The healing of the blind man in John 9 also presents a demonstration of human worth. John 9 opens with this, "As He was passing by, He saw a man blind from birth. His disciples questioned Him: 'Rabbi, who sinned, this man or his parents, that he was born blind?'" (John 9:1–2). While both Jesus and the disciples noticed this man, their reactions were completely different. Jesus saw this man and, it would seem, made his way over to him. He was about to heal this man of his blindness. However, the disciples had no such reaction to this man. Instead, they saw him as the opportunity to ask Jesus a question. He was not a man in need of Jesus's healing touch. Rather, he was a catalyst for a theological discussion on sin and disability.

The reaction of Jesus and the reaction of the disciples were contrasted in the opening verse of John 9. Where Jesus saw the opportunity for healing and the revelation of the Messiah, the disciples saw a question and the opportunity for their theological advancement.

These reactions reveal the way Jesus saw the worth of an individual. The blind man, a person with a disability, was not a problem to be solved or a question to be debated. Rather, he was a person who needed his healing touch. While Jesus did address the question posed by the disciples, the healing of the blind man, and the good shepherd teaching that followed, served to instruct the disciples and the religious leaders on the compassion Jesus had for people. He pointed out that he was the good shepherd and that his care and kindness for his sheep would lead him to do what no shepherd had ever done. The good shepherd would give his life for his sheep. The self-sacrificing action of the good shepherd is the ultimate demonstration of the eternal value and worth of an individual.

Jesus and the Replication of Inclusive Leaders

John 5:1–15 does not mention the disciples. In fact, they are not mentioned in the entire chapter. Consequently, anything related to their involvement in the healing miracle of the lame man would be speculative, based on the assumption that they were silent witnesses to this healing. Thus, whatever conclusions could be made regarding the replication of inclusive leaders from this episode would be conjecture. Nevertheless, in this episode the disciples would have seen the healing power of God displayed through Jesus. They would have seen that power at work in a man who never really demonstrated any faith. Thus, there would have been an element of growth in their understanding of faith and healing. The disciples could also have contrasted this healing to other healings, where faith was present and the healing was both physically and spiritually restorative. This contrast would help the disciples realize that involvement with the marginalized and stigmatized of culture was not dependent on a profession of faith. Belief was not a prerequisite for demonstrating kindheartedness toward another human being. While each of these conclusions are projections, they are not beyond the realm of possibilities. Indeed, this healing episode would have provided a teachable moment that other healings may not have presented.

The healing of the blind man in John 9 provides the best opportunity to consider if this inclusive action by Jesus could have resulted in the replication of inclusive leaders. Since the disciples are mentioned in the opening verses of this chapter, they were obviously present for the healing and the ensuing teaching on the good or model shepherd. With this in mind, the consideration of two episodes in Acts reveals that Jesus's inclusive style of leadership was grasped by the disciples. Additionally, they in turn passed it on to the next group of leaders in the church.

Acts 9:43 and Acts 10:6 tell us about Peter's stay in the town of Joppa. Particularly interesting to his stay in this town was his choice for lodging. Both passages tell us that Peter was staying at the home of Simon the tanner. It is easy to pass over that as you conclude Acts 9 and start into Acts 10. Yet, Peter's selection of this man's house as a place to stay was significant. As a tanner, Simon worked with dead animals to produce leather, creating a situation where both he and his house would have been considered unclean. Certainly, he was the kind of person good religious leaders would purposefully stay away from. They would not be in his company or in his house. Peter, having learned the value of an individual from Jesus, did not see Simon's house as such a place. He also must have picked up on the idea that clean and unclean place designations were also suspicious in God's economy. Thus, like Jesus visiting an unclean pool in Bethesda or coming into contact with a stigmatized blind man, Peter did not avoid Simon or his house because of his vocation.

Neyrey advises that a map of personal pollutants also existed during the time of Jesus. These pollutants were the kind of thing that determined if a person was clean or unclean and their classification of holiness. Neyrey lays out seven degrees of uncleanness. At the head of this list is contact with a dead thing. The middle of this holiness classification list is populated by contact with flux, spittle, semen, and urine.[3] These two components factor into the healing in John 9 and Peter's actions in Acts 9 and 10. In John 9, Peter would have observed Jesus using spittle to make a mud compound that he applied to the eyes of a blind man. This action placed Jesus on this chart of uncleanness. Thus, when Peter was in Joppa, he thought nothing of staying with a man whose profession involved touching dead animals. Peter saw firsthand the inclusive element of Jesus's interaction with something considered unclean, and he was modeling that same inclusionary mentality with Simon the tanner. Yet, lest we think that Peter had this perfectly figured out, the thrust of Acts 10 is Peter's dream and refusal to eat food that is considered unclean. God provided instruction on edible foods in order for Peter to get a much broader perspective on that which was clean and unclean. This vision also prepared Peter for his upcoming ministry to Cornelius the Gentile. It is clear, then, that this training in kingdom inclusion was an ongoing process for Peter.

In Acts 8:26–39 we find the story of a man named Philip. He was one of the seven chosen to be involved in the distribution of food to the needy widows. Here, rather than distributing food, he taught and baptized an Ethiopian eunuch. Two things should be noted about Philip's actions in these verses. First, he ministered to an individual who was at the bottom of the wholeness and holiness rankings in the Jewish sociocultural community. Philip offered no complaints or inhibitions as he undertook this ministry. Further, in the verses that precede his interaction with the Ethiopian eunuch, Philip was proclaiming the gospel in Samaria. This was a territory Jesus frequented, but one that most Jewish religious leaders would have avoided. For Philip, the gospel message was one that did not exclude people based on their geographical location or their ranking of wholeness and holiness. Second, it is worth noting that Philip is a second-generation leader in the church. The practice of inclusion demonstrated by Philip reveals that the way Jesus ministered to the

---

[3] Neyrey, 279–80.

marginalized was passed down to the disciples. In turn, these disciples passed it on to the next group of leaders in the church. Thus, Philip did not see it as odd to take the gospel to Samaria or to an Ethiopian eunuch riding in a chariot. Moreover, Philip's decision to baptize the eunuch upon his profession of faith shows something of this new community of believers. This new kingdom of God would not be defined by stigmatizing boundaries that were products of one's heritage or physical condition. Philip, a man who was selected to be a leader, emulated this inclusive message with his ministry in Samaria and his encounter with an Ethiopian eunuch.

Jesus and Boundary Development

Neyrey observes that the Jews believed Jesus and his followers were turning things upside down. However, when the lives of Jesus and his followers are examined, there is not a lawless quality about them. Instead, Jesus pursued an inclusive plan that marked out how people can relate to God. Jesus was not creating chaos or lawlessness in this process. He was reforming a system by drawing new maps instead of abolishing them all together. These new boundaries allowed human beings to clearly see where they stood in their relationship to God.[4]

When Jesus ventured into the area around the pool of Bethesda in John 5, he was rewriting old boundary maps. Thus, there is more to observe than simply the healing of a man who has no ability to get into healing waters. Instead, the full situation challenged the way the sociocultural boundaries organized one's daily life. Neyrey asserts that the social dynamic of Jesus's day was built around knowing precisely what something was as well as where it belonged. This method of categorization meant there were boundary lines for places, people, things, and times. Each of these areas could be mapped out through a ranking system from whole and holy to broken and unholy. These types of maps allowed for

---

[4] Neyrey, 299.

the easy categorization of what was pure and clean and what was polluted and unclean.[5]

With this in mind, we can see how Jesus was rewriting the boundary lines used to gather and isolate the marginalized and stigmatized in one location so society could promptly abandon them there. He was remapping the understanding of disability as a marker for clean and unclean. His presence restored the value of each disabled person gathered around the pool in hopes of healing. Those gathered were not a collection of disabled individuals. Rather, their value was communicated by the Son of God's willingness to be among the group. They were defined not by their disability, but by their humanity. Jesus did all of this during a particular feast time. In other words, he was involved with those who were deemed unclean, in a place that was considered polluted, at a time when the Jewish calendar would be focusing on purity, cleanliness, and holiness. Considered against this backdrop, it becomes clear that there was much more going on than simply the healing of a lame man. Jesus was recognizing old maps and rewriting the boundary lines in inclusive ways.

In remapping these boundaries Jesus was pointing to a particular relationship that can establish holiness. Neyrey reasons that this idea is reflected in the heart of Stephen's speech in Acts 7. Here Stephen articulated that Jesus Christ, the cornerstone that was rejected, was the new center of the map and of all holiness. Therefore, holiness of place based on one's proximity to the temple had been replaced by a holiness of place that was measured by closeness to Christ.[6] The result of this remapping was an inclusive kingdom where holiness was not tied to a person's ability to gather in the temple complex. Instead, people like the lame man at the pool of Bethesda were given the opportunity to join in this kingdom and know the blessings of physical and spiritual renewal. Sadly, the lame man in John 5 accepted the physical restoration but rejected the spiritual restoration.

---

[5] Neyrey, 274–89.
[6] Neyrey, 292–93.

The good, or model, shepherd teaching of John 10 directly follows the healing of the man born blind. This healing miracle and its accompanying instruction also speak to Jesus's perspective on boundaries. Using a metaphor that involves sheep, a shepherd, and sheep pens, Jesus presented a picture of the recognition of existing boundaries and the institution of new boundaries. In the first segment of teaching, Jesus stated that the shepherd calls to his sheep and brings them out of the sheep pen (John 10:3–4). Jesus used this metaphor to illustrate that he was leading his sheep out of the sheep pen of Judaism and into the freedom of following the good shepherd. Jesus pointed out that in this new boundary development the sheep hear the voice of the shepherd, know the voice of the shepherd, and follow the voice of the shepherd. Thus, they willfully follow the leading of the shepherd out of the boundaries of the sheep pen and into the fields of provision.

When the Pharisees failed to understand his illustration, Jesus elaborated by pointing to himself as the gate to the sheep who are secure in this new sheepfold. Additionally, he called himself the good shepherd. As the good shepherd, it was he who led his sheep both out of the pen into provision and then back safely into the sheep fold. This good shepherd discourse paints a picture of following Christ as a movement within new boundaries. The good shepherd is the one who is the protective gate for his sheep. This new sheepfold affords his sheep with the protection of boundaries established by the good shepherd. However, there is a sense that as the sheep go out of the pen, follow the good shepherd, and then return to the pen, they are still surrounded by the boundaries established by the good shepherd. The sheep are never beyond the watchful eye and caring arms of the good shepherd. Thus, whether Jesus is the gate or the good shepherd, he is the boundary lines of protection and provision for his sheep.

Our Open-Armed Savior

In Acts 10:34–35 Peter proclaims, "Now I really understand that God doesn't show favoritism, but in every nation the person who fears Him and does righteousness is acceptable to Him." Later, while gathered at the

Jerusalem council to discuss the growing Gentile acceptance of the gospel, Peter said, "And God, who knows the heart, testified to them by giving the Holy Spirit, just as He also did to us. He made no distinction between us and them, cleansing their hearts by faith" (Acts 15:8–9). As the disciples took the gospel message into the world, they practiced an inclusive message that they saw initiated in the life and work of Jesus Christ. They did not distinguish between Jews and Gentiles, the physically capable or the disabled, those who could see and those who were blind. They had a map reworked by their Master, and they understood that in his kingdom the marginalized, stigmatized, and excluded were welcomed with open arms.

12

Disability-Inclusive Models of Church Ministry

In *Moral Letters*, Stoic philosopher Lucius Annaeus Seneca wrote, "Our plans for the future descend from the past."[1] Seneca was writing about the value of evaluation and self-reflection. He was convinced that if one paid attention to his or her past, one would become a better individual in the future. Indeed, Seneca seems to attribute a lack of positive progress to the failure of properly considering what can be learned from the past.

When one examines the church's past efforts in disability ministry, there are three initial observations that can be made. First, the church has a history of having some measure of concern for those who are disabled. This care can be traced to both the ministries of the church and the literature of the church. However, this care is easier to review when it comes to examining the existing historical literature on disability ministry. Most of this material expresses only what the church was doing in the past. Little attention is

---

[1] Ryan Holiday, *The Daily Stoic: 366 Meditations on Wisdom, Perseverance, and the Art of Living* (New York: Penguin Random House, 2016), 37.

given to the how and why of disability ministry. Further, the material seems more focused on mental disabilities rather than physical disabilities. One curious observation can be made about this historical material. It would seem there was a consistent number of disability ministry resources published up until the early 1980s. However, the trail of useable content tends to taper off by about the mid-point of that decade. It has only been recently that there has been an uptick in disability ministry resources.

Second, most of the content that was published was not programmatic in nature. By this I mean that disability ministry appears to be something that was an "add-on" to already existing programs. Thus, rather than thinking through ways to involve the disabled into the full body life of the church, the focus was more on things like how to have a Sunday school class for the disabled.

This minimalistic approach to disability ministries highlights one other initial observation about those early days of disability ministry. Material designed to help churches that engaged in disability ministry appear to be singularly focused on the disabled individual. Consequently, very little attention is given to how disability has touched every member of the family. This should not be surprising because church ministry is often programmed toward the individual rather than toward the family. Disability ministry is family ministry, and churches that want to successfully engage in disability ministry today would do well to learn how to intentionally minister to families even as they practice an individualistic ministry that is divided by age and sex.

Disability Ministry: Of Models and Movements

As disability ministry makes inroads into the church, there are various models employed to accomplish this ministry. Further, there is a movement from exclusivity to inclusivity that underlines the direction of the church that engages in disability ministry. A pastor looking for direction in establishing disability ministry must begin by making sense of both the movement and the models of disability ministry. The goal of this chapter is to identify, describe, and organize the models and movement within disability ministry so that they can be structured into one workable model in church ministry. This model will reflect the inclusive ministry modeled by Jesus Christ as presented in the study of the Synoptic Gospels and the Gospel of John.

Historical Models

Disability ministry is not a new concept in church ministry. There are a few older resources that provide models of disability ministry. These models should be noted for the way they propose that the church should engage those who have a disability. Often these historical models focus intently on mental disabilities rather than physical disabilities. However, these models are broad enough that they can encompass ministry to all types of disabilities.

Elmer L. Towns and Roberta L. Groff argue that effective disability ministry should be structured in such a way that it addresses the five main need categories of those who are disabled. These categories are chronological age, physical needs, mental needs, social needs, and emotional needs. Additionally, they postulate that if the student is integrated in a regular classroom for scholastic education, they should also be included in a similar classroom at church. Towns and Groff believe that students' acceptance in academic circles will translate into acceptance within the sphere of church ministry.[2]

Doris D. Monroe demonstrates that there are three ways that provision can be made for the disabled in church ministry. Provision can be made through the regular departments of the church or special classes within the regular church departments, or a separate department or departments can be established to minister successfully to the disabled. She argues for inclusion in a regular department, where there is a sense of belonging for the disabled individual. Additionally, Monroe believes that if others interact in such a way that there is an observable level of acceptance and respect

---

[2] Elmer L. Towns and Roberta L. Groff, *Successful Ministry to the Retarded* (Chicago: Moody, 1972), 52–53.

for the disabled individual, the regular church department should be used to facilitate disability ministry. When considering a special class within a department, Monroe notes the advantages of things like adaptable curriculum, special techniques, and learning aids as reasons to pursue this model. Finally, a separate department should be considered when disability issues cause individuals to stand out from others or they are unable to participate successfully in the activities of the group.[3]

Gene Nabi emphasizes only two possible models for disability ministry. These two options are either mainstreaming or separate departments. He understands mainstreaming as the effort to successfully integrate those with disabilities into the community with other members. For Nabi, the ideal church ministry to the disabled will be one of mainstreaming rather than creating a separate department. Mainstreaming should be considered if the disabled individual is not disruptive, the teacher possesses a general knowledge regarding working with the disabled, and the other students are aware of and accepting of the disabled individual.[4]

Four things become apparent when studying these historical models. First, the concept of disability ministries is not a new programmatic consideration. The church's involvement in reaching out to the disabled is a need that has been previously recognized and embraced. However, it is not a ministry that seems to have had a purposeful continuation.

Second, the models of ministry provided often lack a comprehensive biblical or philosophical foundation. These models are presented as a means of providing care for those with a disability when they are in attendance on a Sunday morning. No mention is provided for additional means of ministry or how this disability ministry would fit within the framework of a specific local church. Additionally, there is minimal use of Scripture to provide a biblical foundation for disability ministry. Thus, the nature of the material

---

[3] Doris D. Monroe, *A Church Ministry to Retarded Persons* (Nashville: Convention, 1972), 42–46.

[4] Gene Nabi, *Ministering to Persons with Mental Retardation and Their Families* (Nashville: Convention, 1985), 94.

can sound more clinical or calculated rather than compassionate. It presents a way to solve a ministry issue rather than minister to a disabled individual.

Third, there are obvious similarities to current approaches of disability ministry. These similarities underscore the reality that few resources have been given to considering how those who are disabled can be valued members of a community of faith. Few churches would consider implementing ministry programs and structures that are more than forty years old. Yet, a lack of attention to disability-related issues shows that current church ministry is relying on these dated models rather than rethinking how disability ministry can lead to inclusion into the full body life of the church.

Finally, none of these historical models calls for direct pastoral leadership. Indeed, a pastor could simply delegate disability ministry to have the program become part of congregational life. These basic models neither require a pastor to be involved nor to be the one who champions the cause of the disabled so that the congregation will rally to their assistance. One wonders if this lack of strong church leadership created the gap between what was being attempted numerous years ago and what is finally being attempted today.

Current Models

The recent collection of literature on disability ministries has produced material that proposes programmatic plans for engaging the disabled who attend church. These new resources pick up where their predecessors left off. Whether in multiple chapters or a single chapter, they seek to disclose how a church can effectively minister to those who are disabled. While the material may be new, most of the ideas presented are similar in concept or approach.

In her discussion on making Christ accessible, Julie Bohn looks at the available options for inclusion. She specifically singles out how Sunday school, Bible classes, and the worship services can be meaningful worship opportunities for children with a disability. She believes that the use of a "worship buddy" is the way to create a meaningful forum for sharing the gospel, memorizing Bible verses, or aiding in understanding the meaning behind the worship songs that were sung.[5] Bohn also advocates for the use and training of "personal shepherds" who can aid a disabled child throughout their entire church experience on a particular Sunday. In her estimation, the concept of a personal shepherd works well when there is more than one trained for each child and when training involves the direct input of the child's parents or caregiver.[6]

Bohn's suggestions are not relatively new. They are either similar to something proposed in the historical models, or they are merely adaptations of one or more of these models. Her suggestions are modifications of the mainstream approach from earlier models. What Bohn suggests that is new to the discussion is the creation of space for those who are disabled to serve others. She proposes that, in some church ministry roles, children are capable of serving alongside their parents. Additionally, children should be given the opportunity to serve the elderly and pray for the congregation in a setting that is conducive to their abilities.[7]

In proposing that churches create service opportunities for disabled individuals, Bohn has picked up on something that earlier models have missed. She has articulated the possibility for a disabled individual to both receive and give compassion within their community of faith.

Another difference in Bohn's proposed model is the attention she gives to foundational disability ministry consideration. She addresses issues related to the church's accessibility needs, the vision of a disability ministry as it relates to the local church, as well as awareness concerns within the local church. What is absent in Bohn's work is a consistent interaction with the Scriptures. Her use of the Scriptures is confined mostly to her presentation of God's love for the disabled.[8]

---

[5] Julie Bohn, "Making Christ Accessible," in *Let All the Children Come: A Handbook for Holistic Ministry to Children with Disabilities*, ed. Phyllis Kilbourn (Fort Washington, PA: CLC, 2013), 279.

[6] Bohn, 276–77.

[7] Bohn, 279–80.

[8] Bohn, 268–74.

Bohn has moved the conversation further with this new material. However, the lack of biblical support is a glaring weakness. One place where she could have effectively incorporated Scripture was in her discussion on raising church awareness to disability concerns. Sadly, this section lacks a sufficient use of Scripture, which is a missed opportunity. Bohn could have easily argued for a pastor to build a biblical case for the churches compassion and involvement with the disabled based on the words of Scripture. Without this scriptural foundation, disability ministries run the risk of appearing as a social organization that seeks the betterment of individuals in a program where the Bible is an optional accessory.

One of the most recent contributions to disability ministries literature is *Leading a Special Needs Ministry*. Lee identifies three potential models for disability ministry. These models include one-on-one assistants, self-contained special needs settings, and a hybrid approach. The hybrid approach utilizes both the self-contained and the one-on-one models to best accommodate an individual and their specific needs. This hybrid approach is centered on an accommodation plan that allows for the child to utilize whichever model works best, given the various factors that can impact the day for a disabled individual. Lee argues that, while the buddy approach is popular, it may not do enough to help establish a sense of belonging for the individual. This sense of community and belonging is most often a residual effect of a self-contained special needs ministry setting.[9]

Ultimately, Lee makes two remarks that must be considered with the adoption of any of her three proposed models. First, she asserts that "there is no single way for a church to do special needs inclusion that will please everyone."[10] Second, Lee articulates that "the goal of full inclusion inside a church is secondary to making the gospel accessible."[11] Thus, for Lee, it seems that flexibility and purpose are the two primary concerns for

---

[9] Lee, *Leading a Special Needs Ministry*, 62–65 (see chap. 9, n. 27).

[10] Lee, 62.

[11] Lee, 65.

disability ministry. This type of ministry must be flexible so that it can best work for the various disability needs represented by the community of faith. However, the end result of disability ministry is more than just the feeling of belonging to a community. Instead, disability ministry should pave the road for the gospel to be demonstrated and presented to those who participate.

Lee's proposal of the hybrid method is new to the discussion on disability ministry. It allows for the greatest amount of flexibility given an individual's changing and unique needs. However, Lee also emphasizes that whichever model is employed must be connected to the mission of a particular church. Additionally, she also connects disability ministry to the mission of the church by noting that disability ministry is not about educational or therapeutic endeavors but about creating an environment where an individual can have a relationship with Jesus Christ.[12]

There is an indebtedness in Lee's models to the historical models. However, she moves the discussion further by describing and eventually arguing for a hybrid model. Additionally, her commitment to connecting disability ministry to the mission of the church also places her work ahead of the historical models. Yet, as with Bohn, there is little connection with the Scriptures. Thus, her models are purposefully presented but lack interaction with the Bible that would give them strength and foundation. Lee's work also fails to articulate the significance of a pastor in creating an awareness in the church. This focus is left to the person assigned the role of special needs ministry leader. Thus, Lee's three models are plagued by the two critical weaknesses. They lack sufficient scriptural support, and there is a notable absence of a pastor as champion for the cause of the disabled.

One unique new model for disability ministry is presented in *Accessible Gospel, Inclusive Worship*. Barbara J. Newman, writing from a liturgical or traditional worship service format, calls for the use of vertical habits as a

---

[12] Lee, 49–53.

means of creating an inclusive worship environment. A traditional order of worship contains the following elements: praise, confession, lament, illumination, petition, gratitude, service, and blessing. These eight elements can be accessibly presented when structured as: Love You, I'm Sorry, Why, I'm Listening, Help, Thank You, What Can I Do, and Bless You. This modification presents the biblical foundations for a worship service in terms that are accessible for most participants in a worship service. Newman sees these habits as being tools that extend beyond the church into activities of everyday life. Given proper instruction and examples, those with disabilities can learn how to worship God through the circumstances of their life rather than simply once a week in a church service.[13]

Newman's model has value for five reasons. First, this model clearly represents thinking "outside the box" when it comes to creating an inclusive worship environment. It is not simply an amended or altered version of other existing models. Second, by necessity, it will involve the pastor and other influential church leaders. Since the vertical habits are linked to the worship service, church leadership must be involved with their implementation. Thus, even without saying anything, disability inclusion becomes a vital part of the life of the local church. Third, the vertical habits do not require the hiring of additional staff, the recruitment of more volunteers, or the shuffling of existing programs. A simple tweak or change of language sets the stage for this method of inclusion. Fourth, while the vertical habits use the traditional order of worship and would work best with that format, they are easily adaptable to any style or worship. This makes the vertical habits a useful means of inclusion for any congregation. Fifth, the vertical habits are highly transitory. This means they can be employed by the youth group or children's worship if they have their own services on a Sunday. Furthermore, their transitory nature means that parents can help

---

[13] Barbara J. Newman, *Accessible Gospel, Inclusive Worship* (Wyoming, MI: CLC, 2015), 35–38.

their children understand how these habits can move from Sunday into a lifestyle of worship.

The strengths of the vertical habits model do not mean they are absent of drawbacks. There is reason to be cautious when adopting this model. Employing these habits means that the verbal content of the worship service must be presented in simple terms so that all who are participating in the worship service can understand what is taking place. Simply adjusting the titles to an order of worship or drawing attention to this basic structure is meaningless if what is communicated under sections like Love You, I'm Listening, or Help are unintelligible for those with a disability. A pastor or worship leader must be a gifted communicator who can engage each person in attendance on their level.

Second, it does not give full consideration to those with auditory or sensory disabilities that could be impacted by things like the volume of the music or the lights in the sanctuary. The complex nature of a disability may be prohibitive to employing this model of inclusion. Since the vertical habits take a general approach to creating an inclusive worship environment, they may be a deterrent to a child with autism who responds quite differently in these circumstances than a child with epilepsy.

Movements

As Lee recognized, there is not one particular way of accomplishing a ministry to the disabled that will please everyone. This reality has caused some to think of disability ministry in terms of movements rather than models. One of the more complex understandings of these movements is proposed by Erik W. Carter in his adaptation of materials provided by the National Organization on Disability. Carter sees a movement of fourteen stages that begins with awareness and ends with sharing the story. This progression includes stages that highlight advocacy, accommodation, inclusion, and outreach. He suggests that as a church becomes aware of accessibility issues in their faith community, they begin to look for ways to become more welcoming. This growth in hospitality introduces them to other obstacles the disabled may face in this community and creates conversations that deepen the desire for an inclusive community.[14]

A simpler movement for a congregation to engage in disability ministry is suggested by Steve Bundy in an article titled "Modeling Early Church Ministry Movements." Bundy identifies seven movements a church must undertake to produce a disability ministry that is beneficial to those who are disabled. These seven movements are a "movement from programs to presence . . . a movement from quantitative ministry to qualitative ministry . . . a movement from a ministry of convenience to a ministry of conviction. . . . a movement from being understood to understanding . . . a movement from being important to being available . . . a movement from being heard to intently listening. . . . and a movement from teaching to being taught."[15]

The one key difference between the movements of disability ministry expressed by Carter and Bundy is related to the consecutiveness of each movement. Carter envisions congregations moving from one movement to the next. They continue along this path until they reach the end of the continuum and have the ability to share their story of effective disability ministry.[16] However, Bundy seems to see each of his identified movements in an individualized manner, where there is little or no connection to the one that either precedes or follows it. Thus, each movement ought to be undertaken and accomplished, but no particular order is necessitated.[17]

When consideration is given to both models and movements, there is little wonder as to why the church has been ineffective in constructing a meaningful pattern for disability ministry. The models have changed very little through the years. The movements simply address what actions a congregation should undertake to be effective in building a welcoming and

---

[14] Erik W. Carter, *Including People with Disabilities in Faith Communities: A Guide for Service Providers, Families, & Congregations* (Baltimore: Paul H. Brookes, 2007), 36–38.

[15] Steve Bundy, "Modeling Early Church Ministry Movements," *Journal of the Christian Institute on Disability* 2, no. 1 (2013): 88–91.

[16] Carter, *Including People with Disabilities in Faith Communities*, 36–38.

[17] Bundy, "Modeling Early Church Ministry Movements," 88–91.

inclusive faith community. These two realities are affirmed by Ed Stetzer who took up his own investigation of disability ministry and the church. In a 2013 *Christianity Today* article, Stetzer indicated that word of mouth seems to be the common means for church leaders to learn of impactful disability ministries.[18]

For disability ministries to be effective in the context of a local church, there needs to be a framework that encompasses both model and movement. This framework must also have a solid biblical foundation that fits seamlessly into the mission and vision of a local church. Finally, it is a framework that is connected to church leadership, so that the cause of disability ministry is advocated by one who will help the congregation biblically and ecclesiastically understand the rationale for such ministry.

An Inclusive Leadership Framework for Disability Ministry

In order for a church to be an inclusive community, it will need to model movement that grows from the external to the influential. This movement from exclusive to inclusive is characterized by four different models. The first model is "external" and is focused on the needs of the community. The second model is "internal" and is focused on the needs of the congregation. The third model is "equal" and finds its basis in the understanding of the congregation. The fourth model is an "influential" model that is rooted in the passion of the congregation.

For each of these models, church leadership plays a vital role in helping the congregation both understand their current location and the ways they need to move forward. A pastor serves as the catalyst to keep the biblical necessity of including those who are disabled before the community of faith.

---

[18] Ed Stetzer, "Special Needs Ministries and the Church: Research, Ministries, Links, Leaders, and More," *Christianity Today* (blog), January 18, 2013, http:// www.christianitytoday.com/edstetzer/2013/january/special-needs-ministries-and -church-research-ministries.html. No longer accessible.

Figure 1: Inclusive Leadership: Disability Effective Models of Church Ministry

Model: External	Model: Internal	Model: Equal	Model: Influential
Ministry Method: Evangelism or Relationship building	**Ministry Method:** Relationship building or Worship	**Ministry Method:** Discipleship	**Ministry Method:** Leadership
Focus: Needs of the community	**Focus:** Needs of the congregation	**Focus:** Biblical understanding of the congregation	**Focus:** Passion of the congregation
Scriptural Basis: John 5:1–17	**Scriptural Basis:** Matt 9:1–8; Mark 2:1–12; Luke 5:17–26	**Scriptural Basis:** Matt 20:29–34; Mark 10:46–52; Luke 18:35–43; John 9–10:21	**Scriptural Basis:** Matt 9:18–26; Mark 5:21–43; Luke 8:40–56

 Individual with a disability

Church member or church leader

Figure 1. Inclusive leadership models for disability inclusive ministry as they move from an exclusive model of ministry to various forms of inclusive models of ministry.

He also serves as the one to highlight where the congregation sits as they move toward a community of inclusion. Additionally, he also addresses the next steps that must be taken so that the congregation successfully moves between models of inclusion.

The External Model

The external model of disability ministry finds its rationale in the needs of the community. In this model, pastors or church leaders have taken notice of the number of disabled in the community, and they are seeking to provide some sort of ministry to these people. The focus of this ministry rotates between relationships and evangelism. In other words, there is a desire to befriend those who are disabled and, where fitting, seek to present the gospel at an age-appropriate level.

Scripturally, there is a connection to what the church seeks to do in an external model and the interaction of Jesus with the lame man at Bethesda. In this encounter and the subsequent conversation, Jesus sought to not only befriend the man but to encourage him to come to faith. While this man chose to reject both invitations, he was invited into a relationship that would have influenced both his circle of friends and his faith. Thus, the external model of disability ministry is not simply designed to push for a salvation decision. Rather, it also serves as the entrance point into a community of faith and a life of faith.

Drawing on Echols's five critical characteristics of inclusive leadership, the inclusive pastor will seek maximum participation of individuals by noticing the disability needs of the community and identifying ways that these individuals can be brought into contact with the community of faith. This type of interaction may happen when a pastor realizes that a local group home has very little connection to the churches in the community. To remedy the situation, he seeks a means of bringing those in this group home into contact with the church. One way he seeks to facilitate this interaction is through the organization of a game night at the church for these individuals.

In terms of empowerment, a pastor identifies those within his congregation who may be both gifted and inclined to disability ministry and finds ways to empower them to service. In turn, these individuals, by nature of their gifting, will relate to those who are disabled in a way that empowers them as well. This mutual empowerment can feed both the evangelism and relationship components of this external model of disability ministry. A pastor will also seek to develop a culture that promotes the worth of the individual. He may accomplish this task by developing a sermon series that focuses on issues of identity or the image of God in every human being. Once again, there is a dual role in this type of disability ministry mechanism. On one hand, a pastor will be equipping his congregation with a better understanding of an identity that is rooted in Christ or the implications of the *imago Dei* for humanity. On the other hand, he will be challenging the congregation to minister to those with disabilities who find themselves outside of the congregational walls.

This empowerment is also achieved through teaching and communicating the message of the gospel. Any discussion on the image of God will invariably address the hope of the gospel. Timothy Keller posits that culture, in many ways, points out the daily failures of life. This repeated pronouncement of failure leaves one's dignity crushed and one's soul in misery. However, the gospel speaks the opposite. It pronounces that individuals are loved regardless of what they have accomplished or failed to attain.[19] This gospel hope is good news for those who are disabled. In a culture where they may have been conditioned to question their worth and value, the gospel proclaims they are loved regardless. When a pastor proclaims this gospel message, he is affirming the value of an individual and creating a culture of inclusion within the body of Christ.

Echols also addresses issues related to leadership development and establishing appropriate boundaries. Both issues are important to an external model of disability ministry. With regard to leadership development,

---

[19] Timothy Keller, *Generous Justice: How God's Grace Makes Us Just* (New York: Dutton, Penguin Group, 2010), 106.

as a pastor replicates leaders who will also share the responsibility for disability awareness in the congregation, he is increasing the congregation's effectiveness in reaching those who are outside of the church. In leadership replication, he is not simply duplicating himself. Rather, he is providing disability ministry with another person whose passion for the disabled is fueled into ideas and concepts that will help move the congregation from a solely external model of disability ministry to one that is internal as well. In boundary development, a pastor is seeking to push the prohibitive boundaries of the church walls further out, so that they encompass more of the church community. One way this can be done is through consideration of the accessibility of the church building. The inclusive pastor who is disability-inclusive will be aware of the places on church property that are barriers or boundaries for the disabled. These barriers may be evidenced in an insufficient number of handicap parking spaces, the lack of handicapped seating, or an inaccessibility to all floors of the church building. Regardless of the boundary, the disability-inclusive pastor will seek for a way to remedy this situation.

The external model of disability ministry makes for a suitable place of initiation into disability ministry. Any church can begin at this point, and in doing so will be more inclusive than they were before they started. However, this model should not be both the starting and the stopping point for disability ministry. To be effective, disability ministry must move from external to internal. It must develop a relationship that goes beyond just a couple of meetings throughout the year. A church that engages only in an external model runs the risk of being viewed as simply another caregiver who works with the disabled as a duty rather than from friendship.

Conner suggests that "friendship shows a way of relating to a person with developmental disabilities beyond the medical model of care."[20] The caregiver has a purposeful reason to be there. It is their paid responsibility to look after and meet the needs of the disabled person. Quoting Professor John Swinton, Conner notes that "friendship is voluntary and has

---

[20] Conner, *Amplifying Our Witness*, 40 (see chap. 7, n. 17).

a different priority as the driving mechanism for the relationship. The priority of friends is the personhood of the other and not the illness."[21]

A relationship that underscores personhood is recognition that friendship is being pursued for the sake of the disabled rather than for personal gain. It is a relationship that loves your neighbor for God's sake rather than your own. Thomas Aquinas stated:

> Now the aspect under which our neighbor is to be loved, is God; since what we ought to love in our neighbor is that he may be in God. Hence it is clear that it is specifically the same act whereby we love God, and whereby we love the neighbor. Consequently, the habit of charity extends not only to the love of God but also to the love of our neighbor.[22]

What does it look like to act in this godly love? Webb-Mitchell argues that the basic activities in this godly love go beyond openly worshiping together, attending a potluck meal, or playing youth group games together. To act in godly love means engaging in mutually agreed upon, long-term relationships. These friendships between those with disabilities and those without will need to be open about the beauty and challenges of life.[23]

When this caliber of relationship occurs, a perceptive disabled person will make two important connections. First, they are being befriended not because it is something a person is required to do. Second, the disabled person will understand they are viewed as something more than their condition. They recognize that they are being seen and treated as a person who, like all people, needs to know the love of another human being.

Hans S. Reinders highlights the contrast at hand in these two important connections as one of "doing something for" and "being with." The difference between "doing for" and "being with" marks the crucial distinction

---

[21] Conner, 40.

[22] St. Thomas Aquinas, *Summa Theologica: Second Part of the Second Part* (Woodstock, ON: Devoted, 2018), 113.

[23] Webb-Mitchell, *Beyond Accessibility*, 143 (see chap. 7. n. 18).

between what professionals in social services do for the disabled and the act of sharing one's life with somebody because one has chosen to be with that person. It is the distinction between professional intervention and personal presence. "Being with" is not inspired by professional goals of improvement.[24]

The reason why friendship is such a crucial starting point for disability ministry is due to the stigma of simply being another ministry project. People with disabilities are all too familiar with those who show up for a limited time, interact with them at their own convenience, and then leave, never to be heard from again. For those who are cognitively aware, they know when they are simply the recipients of another person's charity instead of their friendship. Conner expresses a similar thought when he writes, "Too often people choose to 'reach out' to people with disabilities as a 'ministry' or 'service project.' When the program or project has ended, the encounter is on hold until the next meeting."[25]

For disability-inclusive ministry to be effective, the disabled person needs to know and feel that this relationship is not one that will end once the ministry has concluded. A pastor must ensure that the congregation remains connected and engaged in a continual ministry to the disabled in their community. When both a pastor and the congregation do this, they are communicating to the disabled that they have a friend who will walk with them through life and the faith formation journey.

In the end, the external disability model involves turning the attention of the congregation to the needs that are beyond the walls of the church. Eric Swanson and Rick Rusaw illustratively describe this process as helping the congregation move from the aisle seat to the window seat. Drawing on similarities to the flying experience, they note that those in aisle seats are seldom concerned with being able to see what is outside, no matter how much a pilot recommends that his passengers look outside the window.

---

[24] Hans S. Reinders, *Receiving the Gift of Friendship: Profound Disability, Theological Anthropology, and Ethics* (Grand Rapids: Eerdmans, 2008), 336–37.

[25] Conner, *Amplifying Our Witness*, 42.

Additionally, Swanson and Rusaw argue that the pilot always has the window seat and a view to what is going on outside of the plane. Moving their illustration from the airplane to the church, they note two things. First, the church, like an airplane, needs to become aware that all the action is taking place outside of its walls. Second, those who lead the church, like one who pilots an airplane, must do it from the window seat. Church leaders must be people who look out the window.[26]

The Internal Model

An internal model of disability ministry has its focus on the needs of the congregation. This community exigency may also be the starting point for a church that seeks to engage in disability ministry (as opposed to the external model). Disability ministry that originates here is often at the behest of the parents of a disabled child or perhaps an observant member of church leadership. The basic intent of disability ministry at this level is to provide care for the disabled individual so that the parents can participate in and enjoy the worship service. However, disability ministry at this level can also take on the shape of spiritual encouragement or worship depending on the disabled individual. Thus, internal disability ministry is directed to either relationships or worship.

Scripturally, the restoring of the paralytic at Capernaum can serve as the biblical foundation for this model of disability ministry. Each of the biblical accounts of this story (Matt 9:1–8; Mark 2:1–12; and Luke 5:17–26) note how this healing culminated in worship. The paralytic encounters Jesus and comes to know a wholeness that is physical and spiritual. This results in the ascribing of glory to God.

Using Echols's five critical characteristics of inclusive leadership, the role of a pastor would be similar in the internal model as it was in the external

---

[26] Eric Swanson and Rick Rusaw, *The Externally Focused Quest: Becoming the Best Church for the Community*, Leadership Network Series (San Francisco: Jossey-Bass, 2010), 26–41.

model. However, since both the internal and external models can exist as starting points for inclusive disability ministry, a pastor must not adopt the internal model at the expense of the external model. He must help his congregation see both the need inside of the church and outside of the church. He must help them love both those who are members of the congregation and those who are residents of the community. Derrel R. Watkins notes the way these internal and external factors work together:

> It is obvious that if relationships in the church do not reflect love, then the witness to those outside will be ineffective. However, if love is demonstrated in the church and to those outside with the same concrete actions, Christians' witness will be effective.[27]

This love of others, both inside and outside the community of faith, should not be seen as an either/or starting point. One should lead to the other as the place of meaningful engagement in disability ministry.

A pastor who practices inclusive leadership will seek maximum participation by encouraging his congregation to be active in either form of this disability ministry. For those who are compassionate about the disabled community that exists outside the church walls, he will encourage them to build relationships and create faith-developing opportunities. In the end, these two activities may indeed move those outside the church into the church. Thus, they will move from external ministry to internal ministry from relationship and evangelism to relationship and worship. However, he will also encourage those within the church to be intentional in their involvement with the disabled so that they know they are loved and welcomed within the community of faith. In working with both external and internal ministry models, he is maximizing the number of individuals involved in ministry and creating a disability ministry that is most notably inclusive.

Empowering the individual, both those serving and those being served, will also be a consideration of a pastor. He will seek to create ministry

---

[27] Derrel R. Watkins, *Christian Social Ministry: An Introduction* (Nashville: B&H, 1994), 70.

opportunities where those serving the disabled see their actions in light of both church and kingdom dynamics. This reality will allow those who volunteer in this disability ministry to see that they are shaping lives, transforming the church, and building the kingdom. Similar to empowering those who are being served, empowering the disabled creates the kind of atmosphere where they feel welcomed and accepted within the community of faith. They know they belong within the walls of the church. This acceptance into an inclusionary community is empowering. To this end, a pastor who empowers both those who are serving and those who are being served is creating the kind of community where those inside and out will give glory to God for all that he is accomplishing.

The worth of an individual is one element that both a pastor and the empowered volunteer can pass on to the disabled individual who is part of the community of faith. Often the disabled person suffers from a warped perspective of their intrinsic value and how the image of God relates to them. Thomas E. Reynolds notes, "This theme is a perilous topic for people with disabilities, because Christians have often interpreted disability as a distortion of God's purposes, a marring of the image of God."[28] It is because of this kind of attitude that one of the most empowering topics that can be addressed in disability ministry is a proper understanding of what the *imago Dei* means for every human being regardless of ability or disability. Hubach explains why even a basic understanding of the image of God must matter in the spiritual development of the disabled. She quotes a lecture given by theology professor Jerram Barrs:

> Scripture calls us to recognize that everyone we're ever going to meet is made in the image of God—and that means they're glorious. . . . That's to be our first response: to see the glory of a person . . . to see their glory and their dignity as a person made in the image of

---

[28] Thomas E. Reynolds, *Vulnerable Communion: A Theology of Disability and Hospitality* (Grand Rapids: Brazos, 2008), 177.

God and to treasure all the things that are good and admirable and beautiful about the person as a person made in the image of God.[29]

Each person, regardless of their ability, is manifested with glory and dignity. They are beautiful and admirable. Each of these descriptive words represents language that may be unfamiliar to those who are disabled. Yet, a pastor and the empowered volunteers can speak these words of life into the life of one who may have become accustomed to seeing themselves through the lens of disability.

Perhaps the area of most overlap in the external and internal models of inclusive ministry as it relates to Echols's critical characteristics of inclusive leadership is in leadership replication and boundary development. Leadership replication in the external model revolves around training empowered volunteers to become empowering inclusive leaders. Thus, the inclusive pastor who is disability inclusive will seek to identify those who can continue to lead and influence the present direction of disability ministry as well as shape the future of disability ministry. A pastor, or the church leaders, can draw from the pool of inspired and invested volunteers to train and deploy the next generation of disability-inclusive leaders. Boundary development also reflects similar issues. However, in an internal disability model, a pastor may draw on the input of both the volunteer and the disabled attender (and/or their parent/guardian) to address the prohibitive barriers or boundaries.

There are four common boundaries within a church that prohibit a person with a disability from regular attendance and eventual church membership. These four barriers embody the type of boundaries that must be removed to prevent the marginalization of the disabled within the community of faith.

Anderson categorizes these boundaries as architectural and communication barriers, attitudinal barriers, theological barriers, and aspirational barriers. An architectural or communication barrier within a church is a

---

[29] Hubach, *Same Lake, Different Boat*, 45 (see chap. 1, n. 1).

barrier that impacts physical access, hearing, or vision in relationship to the church building. Attitudinal barriers are the preconceived ideas and mental judgments church members have about disability or those who suffer from impairment. These attitudes manifest themselves in some manner so that a barrier or boundary is erected between the church and the disabled person. A theological barrier is one that has been set in place by a church that has either a limited or incorrect understanding of the theological issues as they relate to disability and impairment. Finally, aspirational barriers are ones that disabled people have taken upon themselves due to repeated negative interaction with others. In other words, they view themselves as unaccepted or unwelcomed in a church because the culture generally treats them that way.[30]

Webb-Mitchell summarizes the significance of accessibility and the presence of barriers. He postulates that even though a church has a blue sticker on its window proclaiming it to be accessible, it is neither accepting nor accessible if certain barriers exist.[31] Until a congregation addresses each of these barriers, the presence of a handicapped accessible sticker is meaningless window dressing. A truly inclusive community is one that has purposefully undertaken the task of barrier removal.

The barriers of architecture and communication, attitude, theology, and aspiration must be recognized and removed for a church to be effective in reaching and caring for the disabled. An approach that emphasizes a robust theology of disability would counteract the negative attitudes and perceptions toward the disabled found within a particular congregation. In turn, this theology would lead to the recognition and removal of significant physical and communication barriers that are prohibitive to those who are disabled. Finally, an inclusionary atmosphere within a church would go a long way in reforming any negative aspirational ideals that a disabled person may have taken upon himself or herself.

In Lev 19:14 God warns his followers not to curse the deaf or put a stumbling block in front of the blind. The reality of God's compassion for

---

[30] Anderson, *Reaching Out and Bringing In*, 15–17 (see chap. 9, n. 8).

[31] Webb-Mitchell, *Beyond Accessibility*, 97.

the disabled gloriously shines through this verse. Today, it continues to call out to God's followers and challenges them to cast aside the barriers that are present in the church. The disability-inclusive pastor who is an inclusive leader will strive to create an environment that is boundary free.

A church that takes the internal model of disability ministry seriously, especially as it relates to its existence alongside the external model, is building spiritual capital. Keller considers spiritual capital to be the spiritual and moral influence the local church has on its neighborhood.[32] The disability-inclusive pastor will use and direct this spiritual capital in such a way that it changes the landscape of disability ministries both inside and outside the church.

The Equal Model

A third model emphasizes the equality of ministry between those who are disabled and those who are not. In other words, a person's disability does not preclude them from serving in a ministry-related capacity. When a church embraces this model, they are doing so because of their understanding of Scripture rather than simply the needs of the congregation or the community. The movement represented from the internal model to the equal model is a movement toward discipleship. It is in the equal model that those who are disabled are given the opportunity to serve alongside another member of the church. Thus, this one-to-one interaction can become the catalyst for discipleship and spiritual growth.

Scripturally, both the healing of Bartimaeus (Matt 20:29–34; Mark 10:46–52; and Luke 18:35–43) and the healing of the man born blind (John 9–10:21) serve as the foundation for a model of disability ministry that places an emphasis on discipleship and shared ministry. In both stories, the men who are healed become part of the community of faith traveling with Jesus. Thus, the implication is they are given the opportunity to learn from Christ, grow spiritually, and participate in ministry opportunities as they journey together with Jesus and the other followers.

---

[32] Keller, *Generous Justice*, 118–19.

A pastor who helps his congregation move in this direction and adopt this model is one who prioritizes the participation of the maximum number of individuals and empowers individuals to reach their full potential. These two critical characteristics identified by Echols are closely related in an equal model of disability ministry. Consequently, the empowering pastor is also one who is pursuing the maximum number of participants in the work of the ministry. The disability-inclusive pastor sees inclusive ministry as ensuring that all who express a desire to serve have the opportunity to do so. Yet, it does not stop at simply allowing for service opportunities. Instead, it goes further by creating the kind of church culture that empowers those in service to reach their full potential. They are not simply serving for the sake of serving. Rather, they are serving with a humble heart and an eye toward doing "everything in the name of the Lord Jesus" (Col 3:17).

In an inclusive ministry where those who are disabled are serving alongside those who are able-bodied, there is a tangible expression of the worth and value of the individual. A pastor who demonstrates inclusive leadership is the type of leader whose concern for the disabled is not limited to helping them cognitively understand their worth according to the Scriptures. Instead, the disabled serve alongside others in the community of faith thereby visually affirming their value, worth, and giftedness.

This kind of proper biblical thinking is life-giving news for someone who is conditioned by our culture to see value and contribution as closely tied together. In other words, those who have the greatest amount of value are those who can make the greatest contribution. Hubach writes:

> Our culture often measures personal value as a function of productivity. The degree to which we are able to contribute to society is the degree to which we are valued. In God's economy, however, human value is defined by the Creator himself though the imprint of this image in mankind.[33]

---

[33] Hubach, *Same Lake, Different Boat*, 49.

Webb-Mitchell also echoes these thoughts. He writes that being created in the image of God means we are also created to be imaginative, creative, talented, remarkable, formidable, and bright people who share our gifts, talents, and services to the greater common good of the body of Christ.[34]

This list of attributes should provide a measure of comfort and encouragement for those struggling to see their worth. The gifts and talents that make up who they are reflect the image of God in them. When the disability-inclusive pastor teaches this properly, he helps the disabled individual begin to comprehend his value and significance to God, the church, and the civic community.

The disability-inclusive pastor must also seek to develop leaders who grasp the importance of ministering alongside the disabled. Lee encourages church leaders to develop working relationships with staff members, volunteers serving in church ministry, individuals with special needs, and their families to build a database of potential future disability-inclusive leaders. Further, she asserts that those leaders who are good team players will also make good ministry leaders. In her estimation, a collaborative mentality is important because disability ministry should not be conducted in isolation or be seen as a separate ministry or church-within-a-church.[35]

Similarly, a pastor who is an inclusive leader helps establish new ministry boundaries to facilitate service opportunities for people with disabilities. These new boundaries hold any necessary leadership requirements and any leadership preferences in tension so that those who are disabled can serve their congregation. One such example of this critical characteristic at work is the installation of a man with Down syndrome as a church deacon. Karen Gorter reports that one congregation created the position of assistant deacon to allow a disabled member of their community to serve alongside

---

[34] Webb-Mitchell, *Beyond Accessibility*, 44.
[35] Lee, *Leading a Special Needs Ministry*, 87–92.

other church deacons. This newly created position allowed the young man's ministry to expand from ushering to diaconal matters.[36]

This example demonstrates how church leadership can assess a situation in such a way that necessary boundaries are held in place, while moving other barriers so the community of faith becomes more accessible. A church that embraces the status quo would find comfort in maintaining an already existing ministry reality of ushering. However, a community of faith with disability-inclusive leaders will seek to create further avenues of inclusion without removing appropriate and necessary leadership boundaries. In so doing, these leaders further remove the potential for those who are disabled to be marginalized.

The Influential Model

The fourth and final model of disability ministry is one of influence. In this influential model, ministry is being accomplished through the leadership and direction of a disabled individual. Thus, they may have moved from someone who was originally engaged through an external model into the internal model of ministry. This eventually translated into discipleship and ministry through the equal model. However, not satisfied with this as a ministry conclusion, discipleship included leadership investment. This relationship resulted in the placement of this disabled individual into a leadership position within the church.

At the heart of this influential model is the congregation's passion to be a biblically inclusive community, where they are committed to more than serving alongside the disabled. This inclusive congregation welcomes and encourages leadership from an individual who is disabled. Thus, they see those who are disabled as being as equally gifted for leadership as any other member of the congregation.

---

[36] Karen Gorter, "Church Installs Deacon with Down Syndrome," *The Banner* (blog), January 18, 2011, http://www.thebanner.org/news/2011/01/church -installs-deacon-with-down-syndrome.

This influential role can be identified with Jesus's healing of the woman with the issue of blood (Matt 9:18–26; Mark 5:21–43; Luke 8:40–56). In this encounter, Jesus takes the faith of the woman and uses it as a means to influence the faith of Jairus. It is the life and testimony of this once-disabled individual that Jesus taps into as a means of growing, leading, and moving Jairus further into faith. Through Jesus, this woman becomes a leader in the faith development of Jairus. She is his teacher as Jesus challenges him and says, "Don't be afraid. Only believe" (Mark 5:36).

The disability-inclusive pastor who practices inclusive leadership will see this influential model as the culmination of Echols's five critical characteristics. Inclusive church leadership that is disability inclusive will seek to involve the maximum number of people and empower individuals to reach their full potential. Thus, a pastor is not simply trying to fill a staff or leadership role with a disabled individual as merely a token of inclusivity. Rather, he seeks out and encourages church leadership to embrace those with disabilities wherever they are best suited to lead a congregation.

A pastor is also the one paying attention to those in the equal model who have been gifted for leadership. His awareness of, and familiarity with, their service allows for him to empower these individuals to move forward from discipleship to leadership. This empowerment encourages their leadership of others as they move from being discipled to discipling others.

Michael S. Beates argues that this type of leader will demonstrate two character qualities. The disability-inclusive leader will be both promoting and multiplying. As an agent of promotion, a pastor "prepares and equips people with disabilities to seek out leadership opportunities in ministry." As an agent for multiplication, a pastor "seeks opportunities to multiply the number of disability-effective leaders in his or her area of influence."[37]

Inclusive leadership, as directed through a pastor, operates in such a way as to have leaders who model individual worth through their understanding of the *imago Dei* and identity. When church leadership is represented by

---

[37] Michael S. Beates, *Disability and the Gospel: How God Uses Our Brokenness to Display His Grace* (Wheaton, IL: Crossway, 2012), 138.

individuals with a disability, it influences the perception of both community and leadership. This type of inclusive leadership subtly communicates a community value of vulnerability and acceptance. Jean Vanier reveals what this kind of community looks like:

> A community is not an abstract ideal. We are not striving for perfect community. Community is not an ideal; it is people. It is you and I. In community, we are called to love people just as they are with their wounds and their gifts, not as we would want them to be. Community means giving them space, helping them to grow. It means also receiving from them so that we too can grow. It is giving each other freedom; it is giving each other trust; it is confirming but also challenging each other.[38]

This type of community can only be achieved when the leadership, regardless of abilities, understands who they are as the image of God. Thus, church leadership shares a common value of the worth of the individual because of the *imago Dei*. This shared understanding of value translates into a free and life-giving community. Both leaders and followers understand how God sees them and how God sees others within the community. Just as Jesus used the faith of the woman to shape the faith of Jairus, so church leadership uses their understanding of individual worth to shape the identity and life-giving faith of the congregation.

The final two critical characteristics of inclusive leadership, as proposed by Echols, emphasize leadership replication and appropriate boundary development to prevent marginalization. These two characteristics seem obvious in the influential model of disability ministry since the leader is one who has a disability. With regard to leadership replication, the disability-inclusive leader has, in a sense, exceeded the element represented by this particular characteristic. Rather than replicating a disability-inclusive leader, he has replicated a leader who has a disability and can continue to keep disability

---

[38] Jean Vanier, *From Brokenness to Community,* The Wit Lectures (New York: Paulist, 1992), 35–36.

issues in the forefront of the congregation. Church leadership that includes a team member who has a disability is a demonstration of the development of appropriate boundaries that prevent the marginalization of the disabled. When the disability-inclusive pastor pursues inclusive leadership so that an individual with a disability is considered for his or her giftedness rather than marginalized for their disability, this pastor is both removing old boundary lines and establishing ones that are biblically based.

David Deuel identifies two ways that leadership replication can happen within a church. First, he believes that leadership replication is a matter of selecting people with disabilities who will provide strength for a church that is suffering. This selection of leaders should involve consideration of gifting and learning. When considering gifting, Deuel encourages viewing these potential leaders in light of the way that God has already prepared and gifted these individuals. These gifts are typically on display in areas where they are presently serving. The consideration of learning is focused on suffering, specifically, what these future leaders have learned through suffering that is beneficial for those presently experiencing suffering.[39]

Second, Deuel believes preparing young leaders with disabilities will require current church leaders to take action. The successful replication of disability-inclusive church leaders will necessitate pastors and church leaders who remove obstacles that hinder young leaders and open doors of opportunity for young disabled leaders.[40]

Deuel believes there are three kinds of obstacles current church leaders must remove. One type is a biblical or theological obstacle. This hindrance is best represented by those who presuppose those priestly prohibitions for disability should still be a leadership consideration today. A social hindrance is another type of obstacle that must be removed. This hindrance assumes that disability is communicable. Therefore, prevention is best achieved by limiting exposure to disability. While this belief is certainly not the case in

---

[39] David Deuel, "Developing Young Leaders with Disabilities: A Ministry Beyond Our Wildest Dreams," *Lausanne Global Analysis* 5, no. 1 (2016): 24–25.

[40] Deuel, 25.

every social structure, it is one that must be cast aside wherever it is found. The final obstacle can be understood as an ideological one. This barrier is erected by those who suppose that the disabled are unable to care for themselves. Therefore, they are unfit to lead others.[41]

In light of these barriers, it is Deuel's contention that current church leaders must open doors of opportunity for the disabled to become leaders. These doors are open by way of training, experience, and assistance in using their spiritual gifts in a leadership capacity. Further, the promotion of capable leaders who have a disability also opens the door of opportunity.[42]

There is a noticeable synergy in Deuel's two ideas of selecting and preparing those who have a disability for leadership. These two ideas fit nicely within the critical characteristics of inclusive leadership presented by Echols. Leadership replication and boundary redevelopment fit hand in glove. As reflected in Deuel's propositions, for leaders to be selected and prepared, it will involve the removal of boundaries and the establishment of ones that are biblically correct. These new boundary lines prevent the marginalization of those who are disabled. Thus, setting the stage so they can be effective leaders within the community of faith. The disability-inclusive leader, who is himself disabled, is one who influences the faith of every member of the church, regardless of their ability or inability.

Conclusion

In Rev 3:14–22 God addresses the church of Laodicea. One of his charges against them is that they are neither hot nor cold. This accusation is tied to the problematic water quality of Laodicea. This city required water to be brought in from outside towns to meet the needs of the community. Through a series of stone pipes, therapeutic hot water was channeled in from the warm healing springs of Hierapolis. Similarly, refreshing, pure, and cold water was also channeled in through stone pipes from Colossae.

---

[41] Deuel, 24–26.

[42] Deuel, 26.

When the water arrived in Laodicea it was neither hot nor cold. It was disgustingly lukewarm. The cultural imagery wrapped into this charge is that God found the Laodicean church to be neither healing nor refreshing. They were nauseatingly tepid and of no use to the culture around them that desperately needed the healing and refreshment a grace-filled community should provide.

It would seem a similar message could be brought to many a contemporary church that has failed to be either a place of healing or refreshment to those who are disabled. Instead, their care for and acceptance of the disabled is simply an indifferent approach that seeks assimilation only when it is convenient for them. A church that takes both the Great Commandment and the Great Commission seriously will be one that is disability friendly. More than that, the disability-inclusive pastor will, through inclusive leadership, encourage the church to move from an external model of disability ministry to an influential model of disability ministry. When this movement between models occurs, the church will be known by its internal love for those in the congregation as well as its love for the community that surrounds the church.

BIBLIOGRAPHY

Akin, Daniel L. *Exalting Jesus in Mark*. Edited by David Platt, Daniel L. Akin, and Tony Merida. Nashville: B&H, 2014.

Anderson, David W. *Reaching Out and Bringing In: Ministry to and with Persons with Disabilities*. Bloomington, IN: WestBow, 2013.

Aquinas, St. Thomas. *Summa Theologica: Second Part of the Second Part*. Woodstock, ON: Devoted, 2018.

Bailey, Kenneth E. *Jesus through Middle Eastern Eyes: Cultural Studies in the Gospels*. Downers Grove, IL: IVP Academic, 2008.

————. *The Good Shepherd: A Thousand-Year Journey from Psalm 23 to the New Testament*. Downers Grove, IL: InterVarsity, 2014.

Beasley-Murray, George R. *John*. Word Biblical Commentary. Nashville: Thomas Nelson, 1999.

Beates, Michael S. *Disability and the Gospel: How God Uses Our Brokenness to Display His Grace*. Wheaton, IL: Crossway, 2012.

Bennema, Cornelis. *Encountering Jesus: Character Studies in the Gospel of John*. 2nd ed. Minneapolis: Fortress, 2014.

Blackaby, Henry T., and Richard Blackaby. *Spiritual Leadership: Moving People on to God's Agenda*. Nashville: B&H, 2001.

Blackwood, Rick. *The Power of Multi-Sensory Preaching and Teaching: Increase Attention, Comprehension, and Retention*. Grand Rapids: Zondervan, 2008.

Blight, Richard C. *An Exegetical Summary of Luke 1–11*. 2nd ed. Exegetical Summaries. Dallas: SIL International, 2008.

Block, Jennie Weiss. *Copious Hosting: A Theology of Access for People with Disabilities*. New York: Continuum, 2002.

Blomberg, Craig L. *Matthew*. New American Commentary. Vol. 22. Nashville: Broadman, 1992.

Bock, Darrell L. *Luke*. Baker Exegetical Commentary on the New Testament. Vol. 3. Grand Rapids: Baker, 1994.

Bohn, Julie. "Making Christ Accessible." In *Let All the Children Come: A Handbook for Holistic Ministry to Children with Disabilities,* edited by Phyllis Kilbourn, 267–85. Fort Washington, PA: CLC, 2013.

Borchert, Gerald L. *John 1–11*. New American Commentary. Vol. 25a. Nashville: B&H, 1996.

Bovon, François. *Luke*. Hermeneia. Minneapolis: Fortress, 2002.

Branch, Robin. "Literary Comparisons and Contrasts in Mark 5:21–43." In *Die Skriflig/In Luce Verbi* 48 (March 20, 2014). https://doi.org/10.4102/ids.v48i1.1799.

Brault, Matthew W. "Americans with Disabilities: 2010." *Current Population Reports*, P70–131, U.S. Census Bureau, July 2012. https://www2.census.gov/library/publications/2012/demo/p70-131.pdf.

Brooks, James A. *Mark*. New American Commentary. Vol. 23. Nashville: Broadman, 1991.

Browne, Stanley G. and Christian Medical Fellowship. *Leprosy in the Bible*. London: Christian Medical Fellowship, 1979.

Bundy, Rev. Steve. "Modeling Early Church Ministry Movements." *Journal of the Christian Institute on Disability* 2, no. 1 (2013): 85–92.

Burge, Gary M. *John*. NIV Application Commentary. Grand Rapids: Zondervan, 2000.

Byzek, Josie. "Jesus and the Paralytic, the Blind, and the Lame: A Sermon." *The Ragged Edge* 21, no. 6 (2000): 23–26.

Calduch-Benages, Nuria. *Perfume of the Gospel: Jesus' Encounters with Women*. Roma: Gregorian & Biblical, 2012.

Carmeli, Abraham, Roni Reiter-Palmon, and Enbal Ziv. "Inclusive Leadership and Employee Involvement in Creative Tasks in the Workplace: The Mediating Role of Psychological Safety." *Creativity Research Journal* 22, no. 3 (August 12, 2010): 250–60. https://doi.org /10.1080/10400419.2010.504654.

Carson, D. A. *The Gospel According to John.* Grand Rapids: Eerdmans, 1991.

Carter, Erik W. *Including People with Disabilities in Faith Communities: A Guide for Service Providers, Families, & Congregations.* Baltimore: Paul H. Brookes, 2007.

Comfort, Philip Wesley, and Wendell C. Hawley. *Opening John's Gospel and Epistles.* Carol Stream, IL: Tyndale, 2009.

Conner, Benjamin T. *Amplifying Our Witness: Giving Voice to Adolescents with Developmental Disabilities.* Grand Rapids: Eerdmans, 2012.

Cooper, Rodney. *Mark.* Holman New Testament Commentary. Vol. 2. Nashville: B&H, 2000.

Deuel, David. "Developing Young Leaders with Disabilities: A Ministry Beyond Our Wildest Dreams." *Lausanne Global Analysis* 5, no. 1 (2016): 22–28.

———. "God's Story of Disability." *Journal of the Christian Institute on Disability* 2, no. 2 (October 1, 2013): 81–96.

Dodd, C. H. *The Interpretation of the Fourth Gospel.* Cambridge: Cambridge University, 1953.

Draycott, Jane. "Reconstructing the Lived Experience of Disability in Antiquity: A Case Study from Roman Egypt." *Greece & Rome* 62, no. 2 (October 2015): 189–205. https://doi.org/10.1017 /S0017383515000066.

Duvall, J. Scott, and J. Daniel Hays. *Grasping God's Word: A Hands-On Approach to Reading, Interpreting, and Applying the Bible.* 3rd ed. Grand Rapids: Zondervan Academic, 2012.

Echols, Steve. "Transformational/Servant Leadership: A Potential Synergism for an Inclusive Leadership Style." *Journal of Religious Leadership* 8, no. 2 (2009): 85–116.

Edwards, James R. "Markan Sandwiches. The Significance of Interpolations in Markan Narratives." *Novum Testamentum* 31, no. 3 (1989): 193–216. https://doi.org/10.2307/1560460.

———. *The Gospel According to Mark*. Pillar New Testament Commentary. Grand Rapids: Eerdmans, 2002.

Eiesland, Nancy L. *The Disabled God: Toward a Liberatory Theology of Disability*. Nashville: Abingdon, 1994.

Erwin, E. J. "The Philosophy and Status of Inclusion." *Envision: A Publication of Lighthouse National Center for Vision and Child Development* 1 (1993): 3–4.

Eve, Eric. *The Jewish Context of Jesus' Miracles*. Journal for the Study of the New Testament Supplement, No. 231. Sheffield, UK: Sheffield Academic, 2002.

Focant, Camille. *The Gospel According to Mark: A Commentary*. Eugene, OR: Pickwick, 2012.

France, R. T. *The Gospel of Mark*. New International Greek Testament Commentary. Grand Rapids: Eerdmans, 2002.

Fredriksen, Paula. "Did Jesus Oppose the Purity Laws?" *Bible Review* 11, no. 3 (1995): 42–45.

Fuhr, Richard Alan, and Andreas J. Köstenberger. *Inductive Bible Study: Observation, Interpretation, and Application Through the Lenses of History, Literature, and Theology*. Nashville: B&H Academic, 2016.

Gangel, Kenneth O. *John*. Nashville: B&H, 2000.

Garland, David E. *Mark*. NIV Application Commentary. Grand Rapids: Zondervan Academic, 1996.

Gorter, Karen. "Church Installs Deacon with Down Syndrome." *The Banner* (blog), January 18, 2011. http://www.thebanner.org/news/2011/01/church-installs-deacon-with-down-syndrome.

Gosbell, Louise. "'The Poor, the Crippled, the Blind, and the Lame': Physical and Sensory Disability in the Gospels of the New Testament." PhD diss. Macquarie University, 2015. http://hdl.handle.net/1959.14/1107765.

Green, Joel B., ed. *Dictionary of Jesus and the Gospels*. 2nd ed. Downers Grove, IL: IVP Academic, 2013.

————. *The Gospel of Luke*. New International Commentary on the New Testament. Grand Rapids: Eerdmans, 1997.

Guelich, Robert A. *Mark*. Word Biblical Commentary. Vol. 34a. Waco, TX: Word Books, 1989.

Haenchen, Ernst. *John: A Commentary on the Gospel of John*. Hermeneia. Vol. 2. Philadelphia: Fortress, 1984.

Hagner, Donald A. *Matthew 1–13*. Word Biblical Commentary. Vol. 33a. Dallas: Word Books, 1993.

Harris, Murray J. *John*. Exegetical Guide to the Greek New Testament. Nashville: B&H Academic, 2015.

Hendriksen, William. *Exposition of the Gospel According to Mark*. Baker New Testament Commentary. Grand Rapids: Baker, 1975.

————. *Exposition of the Gospel According to John*. Vol. 1. Baker New Testament Commentary. Grand Rapids: Baker, 1953.

————. *Exposition of the Gospel According to Matthew*. Baker New Testament Commentary. Grand Rapids: Baker, 1973.

————. *Exposition of the Gospel According to Luke*. Baker New Testament Commentary. Grand Rapids: Baker, 1978.

Holiday, Ryan. *The Daily Stoic: 366 Meditations on Wisdom, Perseverance, and the Art of Living*. New York: Penguin Random House, 2016.

Hooker, Morna Dorothy. *The Gospel According to Saint Mark*. Peabody, MA: Hendrickson, 2009.

House, H. Wayne. *Chronological and Background Charts of the New Testament*. 2nd ed. Zondervan Charts. Grand Rapids: Zondervan Academic, 2009.

Hubach, Stephanie O. *Same Lake, Different Boat: Coming Alongside People Touched by Disability*. Phillipsburg, NJ: P&R, 2006.

Hull, John. "Open Letter from a Blind Disciple to a Sighted Savior." In *Borders, Boundaries, and the Bible*, ed. M. O'Kane, 154–79. New York: Sheffield Academic, 2002.

Jensen, Gordon. "Left-Handed Theology and Inclusiveness—Liberty University." *Horizons* 17, no. 2 (1990): 207–16. https://doi.org/10.1017/S0360966900020168.

John, Jeffrey. *The Meaning in the Miracles*. Norwich, UK: Canterbury, 2001.

Jones, David Lee. "A Pastoral Model for Caring for Persons with Diminished Hope." *Pastoral Psychology* 58, no. 5–6 (December 2009): 641–54.

Keener, Craig S. *The Gospel of John: A Commentary*. Peabody, MA: Hendrickson, 2003.

———. *The Gospel of Matthew: A Socio-Rhetorical Commentary*. Grand Rapids: Eerdmans, 2009.

———. *The IVP Bible Background Commentary: New Testament*. 2nd ed. Downers Grove, IL: IVP Academic, 2014.

Keller, Timothy. *Generous Justice: How God's Grace Makes Us Just*. New York: Dutton, Penguin Group, 2010.

Koester, Craig R. "Hearing, Seeing, and Believing in the Gospel of John." *Biblica* 70, no. 3 (1989): 327–48.

Kok, Jacobus (Kobus). *New Perspectives on Healing, Restoration, and Reconciliation in John's Gospel*. Biblical Interpretation Series. Vol. 149. Leiden, NL: Brill, 2017.

Köstenberger, Andreas J. *A Theology of John's Gospel and Letters*. Biblical Theology of the New Testament. Grand Rapids: Zondervan, 2009.

———. *John*. Baker Exegetical Commentary on the New Testament. Grand Rapids: Baker Academic, 2004.

Lane, William L. *The Gospel According to Mark*. New International Commentary on the New Testament. Grand Rapids: Eerdmans, 1974.

Laniak, Timothy S. *Shepherds After My Own Heart: Pastoral Traditions and Leadership in the Bible*. New Studies in Biblical Theology 20. Downers Grove, IL: InterVarsity, 2006.

Lee, Amy Fenton. *Leading a Special Needs Ministry*. Nashville: B&H, 2016.

Leverett, Gaylen. "Matthew: The Kingdom of Heaven." In *The Essence of the New Testament: A Survey*, edited by Elmer Towns and Ben Gutierrez, 47–63. Nashville: B&H Academic, 2012.

Lioy, Dan. *The Decalogue in the Sermon on the Mount*. Studies in Biblical Literature, vol. 66. New York: Peter Lang, 2004.

Lizorkin-Eyzenberg, Eli. "The Pool of Bethesda as a Healing Center of Asclepius." *Israel Institute of Biblical Studies* (blog), December 1, 2014.

https://blog.israelbiblicalstudies.com/jewish-studies/bethesda-pool
-jerusalem-shrine-asclepius/.

Malina, Bruce J., and Richard L. Rohrbaugh. *Social-Science Commentary on the Gospel of John*. Minneapolis: Fortress, 1998.

Marshall, I. Howard. *The Gospel of Luke: A Commentary on the Greek Text*. New International Greek Testament Commentary 3. Grand Rapids: Eerdmans, 1978.

McNair, Jeff, and Kathi McNair. "Faith Formation for Adults with Disability." In *Beyond Suffering: A Christian View on Disability Ministry*, edited by J. E. Tada and S. Bundy, 470–77. Agoura Hills, CA: Joni and Friends Christian Institute on Disability, 2014.

McReynolds, Kathy. "The Gospel of Luke: A Framework for a Theology of Disability." *Christian Education Journal* 13, no. 1 (Spring 2016): 169–78.

Menzies, Allan. *The Earliest Gospel: A Historical Study of the Gospel According to Mark, With a Text and English Version*. New York: Macmillan, 1901.

Moloney, Francis J. *The Gospel of Mark: A Commentary*. Peabody, MA: Hendrickson, 2002.

Monroe, Doris D. *A Church Ministry to Retarded Persons*. Nashville: Convention, 1972.

Morris, Leon. *Luke: An Introduction and Commentary*. Rev. ed. Tyndale New Testament Commentaries. Vol. 3. Grand Rapids: Eerdmans, 1988.

———. *The Gospel According to John*. Rev. ed. New International Commentary on the New Testament. Grand Rapids: Eerdmans, 1995.

———. *The Gospel According to Matthew*. Pillar New Testament Commentary. Grand Rapids: Eerdmans, 1992.

Mounce, Bill. "A Little Text Criticism (Mark 1:41)," March 24, 2013. https://billmounce.com/blog/little-text-criticism-mark-1-41.

Nabi, Gene. *Ministering to Persons with Mental Retardation and Their Families*. Nashville: Convention, 1985.

Newman, Barbara J. *Accessible Gospel, Inclusive Worship*. Wyoming, MI: CLC, 2015.

Neyrey, Jerome H., ed. *The Social World of Luke-Acts: Models for Interpretation*. Peabody, MA: Hendrickson, 1991.

Nolland, John. *Luke. 1–9:20*. Word Biblical Commentary. Vol. 35a. Dallas: Word, 1989.

Olesberg, Lindsay. *The Bible Study Handbook: A Comprehensive Guide to an Essential Practice*. Downers Grove, IL: InterVarsity, 2012.

Olyan, Saul M. "Anyone Blind or Lame Shall Not Enter the House: On the Interpretation of 2 Samuel 5:8b." *Catholic Biblical Quarterly* 60, no. 2 (April 1998): 218–27.

———. "The Exegetical Dimensions of Restrictions on the Blind and the Lame in Texts from Qumran." *Dead Sea Discoveries* 8, no. 1 (2001): 38–50.

Omiya, Tomohiro. "Leprosy." In *Dictionary of Jesus and the Gospels*, 2nd ed., edited by Joel B. Green, 517–18. Downers Grove, IL: IVP Academic, 2013.

Paavola, Daniel. *Mark*. St. Louis: Concordia, 2013.

Packer, J. I., and Carolyn Nystrom. *Never beyond Hope: How God Touches & Uses Imperfect People*. Downers Grove, IL: InterVarsity, 2000.

Patterson, Dorothy. "Woman." In *The Holman Illustrated Bible Dictionary*, edited by C. Brand, C. Draper, and A. England, 1678–81. Nashville: Holman Bible, 2003.

Pilch, John. "Healing in Mark: A Social Science Analysis." *Biblical Theological Bulletin* 15, no. 4 (1985): 142–50.

Piper, John. *Disability and the Sovereign Goodness of God*. Edited by Tony Reinke. Minneapolis: Desiring God, 2012.

Powell, Mark. "Salvation in Luke-Acts." *Word & World* 12, no. 1 (1992): 5–12.

Quasten, John. "The Parable of the Good Shepherd: JN. 10:1–21 (Continued)." *Catholic Biblical Quarterly* 10, no. 2 (1948): 151–69.

Ranish, David. "Church Still Has Work to Do with Unreached People Group." Mission New Network. March 30, 2011. https://www.mnn online.org/news/church-still-has-work-to-do-with-unreached-people -group/.

Raphael, Rebecca. *Biblical Corpora: Representations of Disability in Hebrew Biblical Literature*. New York: T&T Clark, 2008.

Reiling, J., and J. L. Swellengrebel. *A Translator's Handbook on the Gospel of Luke*. Helps for Translators. Vol. 10. Leiden, NL: Brill, 1971.

Reinders, Hans S. *Receiving the Gift of Friendship: Profound Disability, Theological Anthropology, and Ethics*. Grand Rapids: Eerdmans, 2008.

Reynolds, Thomas E. *Vulnerable Communion: A Theology of Disability and Hospitality*. Grand Rapids: Brazos, 2008.

Rhodes, Ben. "Signs and Wonders: Disability in the Fourth Gospel." *Journal of the Christian Institute on Disability* 5, no. 1 (March 13, 2016): 53–76.

Ridderbos, Herman N. *The Gospel According to John: A Theological Commentary*. Grand Rapids: Eerdmans, 1997.

Roach, David. "Why Were People Healed from Touching Jesus' Clothes?," June 21, 2013. https://biblemesh.com/blog/why-were-people-healed-from-touching-jesus-clothes/.

Rooker, Mark F. *Leviticus*. New American Commentary. Vol 3a. Nashville: B&H, 2000.

Ryken, Leland. *Jesus the Hero: A Guided Literary Study of the Gospels*. Reading the Bible as Literature. Wooster, OH: Weaver, 2016.

Satterlee, Craig A. "Learning to Picture God from Those Who Cannot See." *Homiletic (Online)* 36, no. 1 (2011): 45–55.

Schweizer, Eduard. *The Good News According to Mark*. Atlanta: John Knox, 1970.

Sproul, R. C. *John*. St. Andrew's Expositional Commentary. Lake Mary, FL: Reformation Trust, 2009.

Stein, Robert H. *A Basic Guide to Interpreting the Bible: Playing by the Rules*. 2nd ed. Grand Rapids: Baker, 2011.

Strauss, Mark L. *Mark*. Zondervan Exegetical Commentary on the New Testament. Grand Rapids: Zondervan, 2014.

Swanson, Eric, and Rick Rusaw. *The Externally Focused Quest: Becoming the Best Church for the Community*. Leadership Network Series. San Francisco: Jossey-Bass, 2010.

Swindoll, Charles R. *Insights on John*. Swindoll's New Testament Insights. Grand Rapids: Zondervan, 2010.

Swinton, John. "Known by God." In *The Paradox of Disability: Responses to Jean Vanier and L'Arche Communities from Theology and the Sciences*, edited by Hans S. Reinders, 140–53. Grand Rapids: Eerdmans, 2010.

Tate, W. Randolph. *Handbook for Biblical Interpretation: An Essential Guide to Methods, Terms, and Concepts*. 2nd ed. Grand Rapids: Baker Academic, 2012.

Tenney, Merrill C. *John: The Gospel of Belief.* Grand Rapids: Eerdmans, 1997.

———. "Literary Keys to The Fourth Gospel." *Bibliotheca Sacra* 121 (1964): 13–21.

Tolkien, J. R. R. *The Hobbit*. New York: HarperCollins, 2007.

Towns, Elmer L., and Roberta L. Groff. *Successful Ministry to the Retarded*. Chicago: Moody, 1972.

Twelftree, Graham H. *Jesus the Miracle Worker: A Historical & Theological Study*. Downers Grove, IL: IVP Academic, 1999.

Vanier, Jean. *From Brokenness to Community*. The Wit Lectures. New York: Paulist, 1992.

Vincent, Marvin R. *Word Studies in the New Testament Volumes I: The Synoptic Gospels; Acts of the Apostles; Epistles of Peter, James & Jude*. 2nd ed. Vol. 1. Grand Rapids: Eerdmans, 1977.

Watkins, Derrel R. *Christian Social Ministry: An Introduction*. Nashville: B&H, 1994.

Webb-Mitchell, Brett. *Beyond Accessibility: Toward Full Inclusion of People with Disabilities in Faith Communities*. New York: Church Pub, 2010.

———. *Christly Gestures: Learning to Be Members of the Body of Christ*. Grand Rapids: Eerdmans, 2003.

Westcott, B. F. *The Gospel According to St. John*. Grand Rapids: Eerdmans, 1978.

Whitacre, Rodney A. *John*. IVP New Testament Commentary Series. Vol. 4. Downers Grove, IL: InterVarsity, 1999.

Willmington, Harold L. *Willmington's Guide to the Bible*. Wheaton, IL: Tyndale, 1988.

Wilson, Charles Thomas. *Peasant Life in the Holy Land*. London: J. Murray, 1906.

Wilson, Neil S., and Linda K. Taylor. *Tyndale Handbook of Bible Charts & Maps*. The Tyndale Reference Library. Wheaton, IL: Tyndale House, 2001.

Wuest, Kenneth Samuel. *Wuest's Word Studies from the Greek New Testament for the English Reader, Vol. 1: Mark, Romans, Galatians, Ephesians and Colossians*. Grand Rapids: Eerdmans, 1973.

Yong, Amos. *The Bible, Disability, and the Church: A New Vision of the People of God*. Grand Rapids: Eerdmans, 2011.

SUBJECT INDEX

SCRIPTURE INDEX